THE ART OF SETTLEMENT

THE ART OF SETTLEMENT

SETTLEMENT

A LAWYER'S GUIDE TO REGULATORY
COMPLIANCE WHEN RESOLVING
CATASTROPHIC CLAIMS

JASON D. LAZARUS

HOUNDSTOOTH
PRESS

THE ART OF SETTLEMENT
*A Lawyer's Guide to Regulatory Compliance
when Resolving Catastrophic Claims*

ISBN   978-1-5445-0982-2 *Hardcover*
       978-1-5445-0981-5 *Paperback*
       978-1-5445-0980-8 *Ebook*

To all the trial lawyers who zealously represent personal injury victims. These caring men and women make the world a safer place for all of us.

CONTENTS

INTRODUCTION

When I began my career, I realized early on the incredible responsibility I had in advising people what to do with their settlement after being injured. It is an opportunity to have a positive impact on someone's life when they are probably in their most vulnerable state. With what I do, I see many people who have suffered indescribable things. Many have been an inspiration with their spirit to overcome. In serving my clients, my personal values have always been hugely important: being a consummate professional in every aspect of what I do while serving others. Respecting those I come into contact with is absolutely essential. Acting with the utmost integrity and dedication to purpose allows me to get the job done. Finally, and most importantly, I try to do this while being empathetic to the injury victims who desperately need my help after having their lives changed forever. I didn't really understand all of this as keenly as I do now until I became an injury victim myself. It is as they say, you never know until you walk a mile in someone else's shoes. The following is the story of my own personal injury case.

Those who know me well know how passionate I am about a sport I got involved with when I was thirteen years old—cycling. This sport has given me the foundation to be successful later in life and to keep fit as I have aged. After racing competitively in my teenage years, I kept cycling for health and started to race again in my forties. I have always loved the cycling community and what it has done for me. One of the things that I love about the sport is that it is all about who can suffer the most and has the strength to overcome not only mind but body. Exceeding a limit you didn't think you could is an amazing feeling. I know the people who love me and know me best sometimes just don't get it and don't like the risks associated with cycling. For me, I never worried much about the risks of cycling and tried to be careful out on the roads. Nonetheless, I still always recognized the risks especially considering what I do for a living.

Things changed in 2016. On August 2 of that year, I got up at 5 a.m. to get ready to ride with my favorite local cycling group. It was like every other day where I do this before work. When I get out on the bike early in the morning as the sun is rising, I feel this sense of amazement that I can't explain, but I love it. That morning, I remember feeling strong and fast. I had been training hard and was in amazing racing shape. I was probably in the best shape I had been in since my teenage years. On that day, I turned out of my neighborhood and onto a two-lane road with a bike lane, as I always do. I was lawfully riding northbound in the bike lane and had the right of way. As I got to a little plaza where a convenience store and bagel shop was, something happened. I was hit by a pickup truck out of nowhere. I have flashes of the impact seared into my memory, seeing headlights and my internal voice screaming no. I have very few memories from the accident scene after that except the faint memory of lying on the ground and being turned on my side so the blood could flow out of my bleeding face. That was the start of my journey as a personal injury victim, which was quite intense and at times very scary early on.

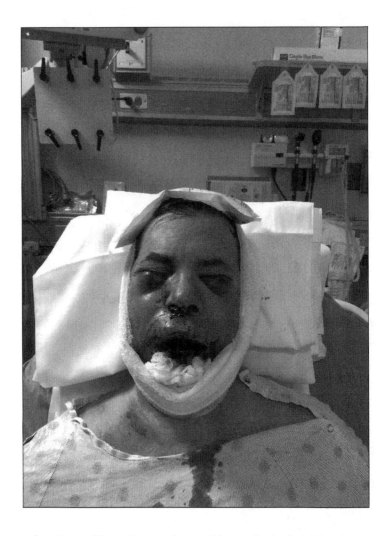

After the accident, I remember waking up in the local, level one trauma center. I knew I was pretty banged up but had no idea the extent of my injuries. I would later learn that all the bones in my face were pretty much broken—I was diagnosed with a Le Fort III fracture. I had a severely broken jaw that was broken in multiple places, requiring a metal plate in my chin. Broken nose. My lower lip had been ripped in half and I had significant dental injuries (seven upper teeth knocked out). I also broke my right clavicle requiring a plate and screws. I spent three agonizingly long weeks in the hospital. Nine of those days were in ICU. When I awoke in the hospital after my medically induced, five-day coma, I found that my jaw was wired shut and I was on a ventilator. I couldn't verbally communicate, since I had a tube stuck down my throat to breathe and a feeding tube. After a week or so, they did a tracheotomy due to the pain that the ventilator was causing my severely broken jaw. During my hospitalization, there were many traumatic moments, most of which were related to having my trach tube suctioned due to secretions. When they do that to you, it feels like you are choking to death since you can't breathe. Once I was moved to a step-down unit and they felt it was safe to remove my trach tube, I was finally able to regain use of my voice. Before I could be released, they had to do a swallow study to make sure I could properly swallow liquids and not aspirate. So almost three weeks after my accident, I could swallow liquids for the first time without a feeding tube.

Once I was released from the hospital, I went home to recover. With my jaw wired shut, I was on a liquid only diet for two months. It took almost two years of dental work, with orthodontics and implants, to return my mouth to a condition where I could eat normally once again. The worst part of it all was the fact that my mouth would never be normal again. Have you ever had a pebble in your shoe that you couldn't wait to get out? Well, that is what it was like with my mouth except I can never remove the pebble. An activity of daily living—eating food was permanently impacted/altered. I can no longer enjoy food the way I used to. As a result of the accident, I lost a lot of time that I won't ever get back. I couldn't work for two months as talking was difficult and nutrition was very difficult with my jaw wired shut. My business had to be taken over by our board of directors who assumed my CEO responsibilities. I couldn't write articles, speak publicly, or do the things I would have done to grow my business. A sport/hobby/investment in my own wellness I love, cycling, was nearly taken away from me. I was able to get back on the bike, but it just will never ever be the same.

While the physical damages were significant, the emotional and psychological damages were equally significant. The indignities suffered in the hospital and the complete loss of control I suffered are scars that couldn't be reversed. I suffered significant post-traumatic stress symptoms and sought counseling to cope with the issues I endured over the two years post-accident. My children had to see me in a condition which no child should have to see their parent in. The rest of my family and friends had to endure not knowing whether I was going to survive. Like many injury victims, I had to figure out insurance coverage issues for my healthcare. Unfortunately, many of my post-accident medical expenses were not covered by health insurance, since a lot of it was cosmetic and dental.

Given all that I suffered, I hired a personal injury attorney (who happened to be a friend) to look into a potential case. I vividly remember him coming to see me in the hospital and having to communicate with a pad and paper because I couldn't speak. As it turned out, the driver who hit me worked at the bagel shop in the plaza where I was hit. He was turning into the plaza to go to work when he hit me. He had the minimum coverage in Florida, a $10,000 policy and that was it. Thankfully, I had quite a bit of underinsured motorist coverage which did cover me. However, they didn't tender the stacked policies even though it was a pretty clear liability. So, like most injury victims, I had to bring suit. I was deposed twice, and the case progressed. We ultimately got a date set for mediation. My personal injury lawyer did a phenomenal job on my case and put it into a posture to settle for close to policy limits. During the mediation opening, I did the damages presentation so I could speak directly to the adjuster. I got the opportunity to look her and the driver in the eye to explain the tremendous impact this had on my life, my family, and my business. The case ultimately settled.

After it settled, I felt the relief and catharsis that mediation can bring to one who has endured months or years of litigation. I also had to make many of the decisions that I discuss routinely with clients and in this book. I had to figure out what to do with my recovery and how to protect myself. I did what I recommend to my clients routinely, I set up a structured settlement and a trust for my future medical expenses. I had to deal with and negotiate my health insurer lien. So, I faced all of the same issues that clients I regularly work with face when their case is resolved. It was an enlightening experience. As a result, I learned intimately what injury victims have already encountered by the time I get the opportunity to work with them. While it is very helpful to have this unique understanding, I would have preferred not to have experienced all that I did. I am sure that sentiment is shared by every other person who has been injured as the result of someone else's negligence.

I do count myself among the lucky in spite of it all. I could have suffered a traumatic brain injury, a spinal cord injury, or even death. I see so many clients in my practice who weren't as lucky as I was. In the end, I am very thankful for being able to walk, talk, and think. The doctors and nurses who cared for me were incredible. I am grateful for the care they provided to me and the other medical professionals who have helped me recover. Also, I am grateful for the tort system that gave me the opportunity to have my damages addressed and the ability to face the person who forever changed my life with his negligence.

While I felt it was important to tell my story of being a personal injury victim first, it is equally important to understand a little about my background, how I came to write this book, and why. Twenty years ago, I embarked on a new career path that has had quite a few twists and turns. At that time, I made the decision to leave a defense litigation practice and put my legal training to work in a different field—settlement consulting. When I started out, it seemed simple enough. Assist trial lawyers when they settle a catastrophic case. As with anything, when you start to peel back the layers of the onion, you learn it is anything but simple. As the years went by in my settlement planning practice, I started to understand how complex it all really is. The intersection of taxation of damages, public benefit preservation, Medicare Secondary Payer compliance, trusts, liens, and the financial options is a niche that I realized was being underserved.

In 2008, while serving as the president of a national settlement consulting firm, the idea of a company that could simultaneously assist trial lawyers with all these areas began to take hold in my mind. At that point, I made the decision to start my own company and build out the model. During this time, I was also finishing up my LLM degree in elder law to continue my training/focus on planning for those with disabilities. Since there is an interconnectivity among all these disciplines, it was a fortuitous decision to pursue my degree while building the foundation for what would become Synergy Settlement Services. Over the last eleven years, the vision has come into focus and the business I envisioned has become a reality.

Day in and day out, Synergy helps trial lawyers focus on what they do best by dealing with the issues that arise at settlement, like lien resolution, Medicare compliance, public benefit preservation, and settlement planning techniques. This book chronicles all those issues and helps trial lawyers navigate the issue spotting that needs to happen in every personal injury practice when settling cases for those who are significantly disabled. Ultimately, it is a guide for personal injury lawyers to help close cases compliantly at settlement.

CHAPTER 1

ETHICAL ISSUES AT SETTLEMENT

Suffering even a moderate personal physical injury can create difficult challenges both financially and emotionally for even the strongest among us. However, what happens when someone suffers a serious or catastrophic personal physical injury? Do they get the proper counsel regarding the form of the settlement to protect their current assets, preserve public benefits, and safeguard the physical injury recovery? Will the recovery be enough to pay for all the victim's future medical needs without public assistance? Can they recover physically? Can they recover emotionally? All these issues can be very difficult to face for someone who is seriously injured. Personal injury practitioners who represent disabled clients should be aware of their obligations to advise these clients properly and understand the hurdles faced by the injury population in terms of recovery both financially and physically. This chapter addresses issues of major importance when dealing with the form of settlement for a personal injury matter involving a disabled client.

THE ABA MODEL RULES AND ETHICAL OBLIGATIONS TO ADVISE THE PERSONAL INJURY CLIENT

Personal injury lawyers are excellent at consulting with clients on the value of their case and obtaining significant monetary results in the litigation, however, the practitioner sometimes fails to properly advise/protect their client financially post-settlement.[1] For personal injury victims there is usually a focus on the dollar amount of the recovery rather than how the recovery can be structured to provide protection to the disabled injury victim.[2] The concentration of substance over form by the lawyer handling the physical injury suit can have devastating consequences for an injury victim. A disabled injury victim can mismanage their personal injury recovery and lose the public benefit eligibility they desperately need.[3] Therefore, questions arise: Does a lawyer have an ethical obligation to advise a disabled client regarding the form of their recovery? Does the lawyer have an ethical duty to explain the impact of a personal injury recovery on public benefits and techniques to protect eligibility? Below I examine the ethical rules, statutes, and case law to shed some light on potential answers to these questions.

There are four provisions within the ABA Model Rules of Professional Conduct that are particularly relevant to the personal injury lawyer's advisement obligations when it comes to consulting on the form or structure of a disabled injury victim's recovery. Rule 1.4 (b) provides: "A lawyer shall explain a matter to the extent reasonably necessary to permit the client to make

---

1   This statement is based on the author's personal experience and observations in countless cases. However, the author acknowledges that practices do vary considerably in this area. Some trial lawyers may simply refer a client to a financial advisor or a local bank. Others may employ a settlement planner with expertise in structured settlements and public benefit preservation techniques. See also Ellen S. Pryor, Liability for Inchoate and Future Loss After Judgment, Va. L. Rev., 1758, 1813–1827 (2002) (concluding that practices vary considerably in terms of advisement by the trial lawyer regarding financial obligations at settlement).

2   *Id.*

3   *See Generally* Marcus L. Plant, *Periodic Payment of Damages for Personal Injury*, La. L. Rev., 1327, 1331–1332 (discussing numerous studies on dissipation of settlements and the resulting dependence on public assistance programs).

informed decisions..."[4] Rule 1.3 states: "A lawyer shall act with reasonable diligence and promptness in representing a client."[5] The commentary warns: "A client's interests can be adversely affected by the passage of time."[6] Rule 1.2 (a) admonishes that: "A lawyer shall abide by the client's decisions concerning the objectives of representation...and shall consult with the client as to the means by which they are to be pursued."[7] Rule 1.2 also says: "a lawyer shall abide by the client's decision whether to settle a matter."[8] Finally, Rule 2.1 indicates: "In rendering advice, a lawyer may refer not only to law but to other considerations such as moral, economic, social, and political factors that may be relevant to the client's situation."[9]

Many personal injury practitioners seem to believe that advice regarding financial matters and techniques to preserve public benefit eligibility crosses the line between legal and "financial" advice. However, as I will discuss more thoroughly below, these issues touch on the law and do create an obligation on the part of the personal injury practitioner to properly advise the client regarding their implication as to the form or structure of the recovery. If you take the Model Rules together with the legal malpractice case law discussed below, it is this author's opinion that the personal injury lawyer must address the financial implications of the settlement and impact on public benefit eligibility with the injured client to enable the client to make an informed decision about the form of the settlement. Allowing a disabled

---

4   Model Rules of Professional Conduct Rule 1.4(b) (2007).

5   Model Rules of Professional Conduct Rule 1.3 (2007).

6   Model Rules of Professional Conduct Rule 1.3 (2007).

7   Model Rules of Professional Conduct Rule 1.2(a) (2007).

8   Model Rules of Professional Conduct Rule 1.2 (2007).

9   Model Rules of Professional Conduct Rule 2.1 (2007).

client to take the personal injury recovery in a single lump sum without any advice on the impact of that decision would set up a situation where the client could be adversely impacted by the passage of time.

MALPRACTICE LIABILITY FOR FAILING TO ADVISE INJURY VICTIM CLIENTS

The *Grillo*[10] case from Texas is the most widely publicized legal malpractice settlement involving liability for failing to counsel a minor client on the form of a personal injury settlement. Christina Grillo was born with cerebral palsy, cortical blindness, and quite a few other medical problems.[11] Her parents instituted a medical malpractice action alleging her medical problems were due to negligent medical care during delivery in a Texas hospital. The medical malpractice case was settled for $2.5 million.[12] The settlement was placed into the court registry.[13] The interest earned from the investments in the trust was taxable and the child lost her Medicaid eligibility since no Special Needs Trust was established.[14]

The personal injury lawyers who handled the case were later sued for legal malpractice for their handling of the settlement. In the legal malpractice action, Grillo's legal counsel, Kevin Isern, alleged that her personal injury lawyer "didn't offer a structured settlement to the child and "[t]hey had the money deposited into

---

10 Grillo was a confidential legal malpractice settlement that became public due to a filing error on the part of the court approving the malpractice action. *See* Amy Johnson Conner, *Is Plaintiffs' Lawyer Liable for Not Offering Structured Settlement? Lawyers Weekly USA* (August 6, 2001).

11 *Id.*

12 *Id.*

13 *Id.*

14 *Id.*

the registry of the court...and she lost Medicaid."[15] Having the money placed in the court registry meant Christina Grillo could not have a tax-free structured settlement and all of the accrued interest was taxable. Isern pointed out that "[i]n a structured settlement, that does not occur."[16] He also pointed to the fact that the lawyers also failed to set up a Special Needs Trust which would have preserved her Medicaid eligibility.[17] Finally, Isern pointed out that in the *Grillo* case "[y]ou have a child who has all these needs, requires 24-hour care and has no government assistance to help pay for it. She got taxed on all the money she gained."[18]

The *Grillo* legal malpractice case was settled by the personal injury firm that handled the medical malpractice action on behalf of the minor and by the guardian ad litem (GAL) who had represented the minor's interests when the settlement was approved.[19] The personal injury firm settled the legal malpractice action for its handling of the medical malpractice settlement for $1,600,000. Interestingly, the suit against the GAL was settled for $2,500,000. For attorneys who serve as guardian ad litems with any frequency, it is attention grabbing that the GAL wound up with the largest share of the liability in terms of the gross settlement amount. However, it sends a clear warning message to personal injury lawyers as well as guardian ad litems about their obligations to properly advise a client about the financial options they have and preservation of public benefits.

---

15   *Id.*

16   *Id.*

17   *Id.*

18   *Id.*

19   Amy Johnson Conner, *Is Plaintiffs' Lawyer Liable for Not Offering Structured Settlement? Lawyers Weekly USA* (August 6, 2001).

The only other reported decision regarding a suit over failing to give advice about the form of settlement is the *French v. Glorioso* decision.[20] In *French*, the injury victim, Karen French, was shot during a robbery attempt at a parking garage in New Orleans and was rendered a quadriplegic.[21] She brought suit against the owners of the parking garage for providing insufficient security.[22] At the time of the shooting, she was covered by a group healthcare plan but subsequently lost the coverage and was dependent on Medicaid. The case was settled in November of 1998.[23] In July of 1999, French consulted an attorney about setting up a Special Needs Trust (SNT). The attorney advised her that she would lose her Medicaid eligibility, since the settlement was deposited into the plaintiff attorney's trust account.[24] Following this discovery, French sued the personal injury lawyer for legal malpractice, negligent misrepresentation, breach of contract, and breach of fiduciary duty.[25]

Ultimately, the *French* case was not decided upon the merits of her claim against her personal injury attorney but instead on a personal jurisdiction issue.[26] Ms. French hired a Texas lawyer to handle the claim, who, in turn, associated with local Louisiana counsel since the suit needed to be filed in Louisiana.[27] The legal malpractice action was brought in Texas against the

---

20   *French v. Glorioso*, 94 S.W.3d 739 (Tex. Ct. App. 2002).

21   *Id.* at 743.

22   *Id.*

23   *Id.*

24   *Id.*

25   *Id.*

26   *Id.* at 747.

27   *Id.* at 743.

Louisiana attorney, which raised personal jurisdiction issues.[28] There appeared to be some factual dispute between French and her personal injury attorney over what had been recommended in terms of setting up an SNT, but this case again demonstrates the potential malpractice liability for failing to properly and fully advise clients about the impact of the settlement on their financial situation and public benefit eligibility.[29]

Finally, the American Bar Association released its report on the *Profile of Legal Malpractice Claims* in 2003 and personal injury lawyers made up the largest percentage of malpractice claims, 20 percent.[30] Advice and settlement/negotiation made up over 23 percent of the claims overall.[31] When those two categories are combined, they are tied for first in terms of the highest claims by type of activity in the study.[32] While the report does not specify, it is logical to conclude that claims of failing to give advice about financial options, taxation of damages, and preservation of public benefits would squarely fall within the purview of advice as well as settlement/negotiation malpractice claims.

ETHICAL AND LEGAL DUTIES TO THE PLAINTIFF AT SETTLEMENT

The fact that all the issues relating to the form of the recovery touches the law drives home the fact that it is the personal injury lawyer's obligation to at least raise these issues as part of their

---

28 *Id.*

29 *Id.* at 747.

30 *American Bar Association Standing Committee on Lawyers' Professional Liability*, Profile of Legal Malpractice Claims (2003).

31 *Id.*

32 Preparation, filing, and transmittal of documents made up 23.08 percent of claims. The next highest claim by type of activity, after the combination of advice and settlement/negotiation, was pretrial and prehearing at 19.47 percent. *American Bar Association Standing Committee on Lawyers' Professional Liability*, Profile of Legal Malpractice Claims (2003).

discussions with the disabled client. As discussed above, there are provisions in the United States Code along with the Internal Revenue Code that impact the form of the recovery. These provisions, if not explained to the injury victim client, can result in the client's inability to avail themselves of options available under the law. If the injury victim's lawyer does not explain these issues to them, who will?

If the disabled client is not given advice about how to structure their recovery, they could suffer quantifiable damages that can be proven in a legal malpractice case. There are many experts that can be hired to make sure clients are properly advised of all their options for their recovery. To avoid future liability, the personal injury lawyer should hire such experts to protect their clients and themselves. If clients refuse counseling or refuse methods to protect their recovery, a good course of action is to have them sign a waiver or acknowledgment that they have been advised of their options and understand what they are giving up. If the personal injury practitioner gives clients all their options regarding how to structure their recovery, and has them sign a waiver/acknowledgment if they decline the options presented to them, the lawyer has at least documented the file so if there is a subsequent legal malpractice claim, they can offer evidence of the advice they gave.

Pursuant to the *Grillo* decision and the Model Rules, a lawyer must counsel clients regarding their financial options and techniques to preserve public benefits to avoid causing a potential loss to the client. *Grillo's* message to plaintiff lawyers is to employ or consult competent experts in taxation, trusts, and structured settlements prior to distributing any funds to the injury victim. If a lawyer fails to discuss the financial options a client has, and then the client sues for legal malpractice, there are demonstrable damages as *Grillo* so aptly demonstrated. Without knowledge of the tax law, the client can lose the power of a significant tax exemption offered for structured settlement recipients. He or she can lose out on the opportunity for a safe investment with competitive rates of return. Finally, and potentially the most damaging, the client can lose public assistance eligibility.

The problem is that plaintiff counsel typically has a very short time period within which to counsel the client in between settlement/verdict and disbursement of the funds. The biggest mistake a personal injury lawyer can make is triggering constructive receipt[33] by placing the settlement proceeds in his or her trust account. One solution to the settlement time crunch is to use a qualified settlement fund (QSF) discussed in greater detail in chapter 17. A QSF is a temporary settlement-related trust that can be created pursuant to Treasury Regulations to receive personal injury settlement proceeds.[34] A court with jurisdiction over the matter must issue an order creating the trust and the trust must meet the definition of a trust under state law.[35] Once created, it

---

33 Constructive receipt is a tax doctrine that says even though a taxpayer might not have actual possession of money, they have constructively received the money if it has been set aside, credited to an account, or otherwise is available without limitation to the taxpayer. Money held in a plaintiff attorney's trust account that belongs to the personal injury victim is constructively received for tax purposes. This concept is important because once triggered, the plaintiff forever loses the ability to structure his or her settlement and could lose public benefits.

34 Treas. Reg. § 1.468B-1 (2007). There are three requirements for creation of a QSF: (1) It is *established pursuant to an order* of...a court of law...; (2) It is *established to resolve or satisfy one or more* contested or uncontested claims...and that has given rise to at least *one claim* asserting liability (i) Under CERCLA (ii) Arising out of a tort, breach of contract, or violation of law; or (iii) Designated by the Commissioner in a revenue ruling or revenue procedure; and (3) The fund, account, or trust is a trust under applicable state law...

35 Treas. Reg. § 1.468B-1 (2007). The mechanical steps involved in utilizing a QSF are as follows: 1. Settle with Defendant for cash and execute a cash release which includes the agreement that Defendant will pay the settlement proceeds into the QSF. 2. Petition a court with jurisdiction for creation of Qualified Settlement Fund and obtain order creating QSF. 3. Defendant writes a check for the net proceeds to the Plaintiff to the Qualified Settlement Fund. 4. Funds remain in Qualified Settlement Fund, without violating constructive receipt doctrine, until: a. Allocation decisions are made; b. Liens are satisfied; c. Special needs trust is created or deemed not necessary. Amount to be structured and the plan are decided upon. 5. QSF automatically terminates when all funds have been dispersed.

allows for an immediate cash settlement with the defendant and removes the defendant from the process. The QSF acts as a holding tank for the settlement proceeds and gives plaintiff counsel time to employ experts while preserving the ability to structure the settlement as well as create public benefit preservation trusts without violating the tax doctrine of constructive receipt. A financial plan can be developed, and the client's needs addressed.

A personal injury practitioner must discuss with disabled clients the form of their personal injury recovery or hire an expert to do so. There are many different options when it comes to the form of the financial recovery. While there certainly is no clear-cut answer as to the amount of the recovery that would trigger the counseling obligation, if a physical injury recovery could result in loss of public benefits, it is prudent for the lawyer to give advice to that client about the options or have an expert do so. Every client, no matter age, sex, or level of sophistication, should be given their options regarding the form of the recovery which are available under the law. Disabled clients especially need counseling, given the likelihood they will be receiving some type of public benefits. To prevent being exposed to a malpractice cause of action, the personal injury practitioner should understand the types of public benefits that a disabled client may be eligible for and techniques that are available to preserve those benefits. Having this knowledge will help the lawyer identify disabled clients they may want to refer for further consultation with other experts.

CHAPTER 2

OVERVIEW OF PUBLIC ASSISTANCE PROGRAMS AND LAWS THAT IMPACT SETTLEMENT

Because most of a lawyer's malpractice exposure at settlement is related to public benefit preservation, it is important to understand the basics of these benefits. Ethically, a lawyer must be able to explain these matters to the extent that the client is informed sufficiently to make educated decisions. There are two primary public benefit programs available to those who are injured and disabled. The first is the Medicaid program and the intertwined Supplemental Security Income benefit (SSI). The second is the Medicare program and the related Social Security Disability Income/Retirement benefit (SSDI). Both programs can be adversely impacted by an injury victim's receipt of a personal injury recovery. Understanding the basics of these programs and their differences is imperative to protecting the client's eligibility for these benefits.

Medicaid and Supplemental Security Income (hereinafter SSI) are income- and asset-sensitive public benefits which require special planning to preserve. In many states, one dollar of SSI benefits automatically provides Medicaid coverage. This is very important, as it is imperative in most situations to preserve some level of SSI benefits if Medicaid coverage is needed in the future. SSI is a cash assistance program administered by the Social Security Administration. It provides financial assistance to needy, aged, blind, or disabled individuals. To receive SSI, the individual must be aged (sixty-five or older), blind, or disabled,[36] and be a US citizen. The recipient must also meet the financial eligibility requirements.[37] Medicaid provides basic healthcare coverage for those who cannot afford it. It is a state and federally funded program run differently in each state. Eligibility requirements and services available vary by state. Medicaid can be used to supplement Medicare coverage if the client is eligible for both programs.[38] For example, Medicaid can pay for prescription drugs as well as Medicare co-payments or deductibles. Medicaid and SSI are income and asset sensitive, therefore creation of a Special Needs Trust may be necessary, which is described in greater detail below.

Medicare and Social Security Disability Income (hereinafter SSDI) benefits are an entitlement and are not income or asset

---

36 Disability is defined the same way as for Social Security Disability benefits which is that the disability must prevent any gainful activity (e.g., employment), last longer than twelve months, or be expected to result in death. If someone receives disability benefits from Social Security, they automatically qualify as being disabled for purposes of SSI eligibility.

37 An individual can only receive up to $552 per month ($829 for couples) and no more than $2,000 in countable resources.

38 This is commonly referred to as "dual eligibility." For those who are dual eligible, Medicaid will pay Medicare premiums, copayments, and deductibles within prescribed limits. There are two different programs. First, is Qualified Medicare Beneficiaries (QMB). The QMB program pays for the recipient's Medicare premiums (Parts A and B), Medicare deductibles, and Medicare coinsurance within the prescribed limits. QMB recipients also automatically qualify for extra help with the Medicare Part D prescription drug plan costs. The income and asset caps are higher than the normal SSI/Medicaid qualification limits. Second is Special Low-Income Medicare Beneficiary (SLMB). The SLMB program pays for Medicare premiums for Part B Medicare benefits. SLMB recipients automatically qualify for extra help with Medicare Part D prescription drug plan costs. Again, the income and asset caps are higher than the normal SSI/Medicaid qualification limits.

sensitive. Clients who meet Social Security's definition of disability and have paid enough quarters into the system can receive disability benefits regardless of their financial situation.[39] The SSDI benefit program is funded by the workforce's contribution into FICA (Social Security) or self-employment taxes. Workers earn credits based on their work history and a worker must have enough credits to get SSDI benefits should they become disabled. Medicare is a federal health insurance program. Medicare entitlement commences at age sixty-five or two years after becoming disabled under Social Security's definition of disability.[40] Medicare coverage is available again without regard to the injury victim's financial situation. A Special Needs Trust is not necessary to protect eligibility for these benefits. However, the Medicare Secondary Payer Act (MSP) may necessitate the use of a Medicare Set-Aside discussed in greater detail below.

LAWS THAT IMPACT SETTLEMENT

In order to properly advise personal injury victims about their legal options at settlement, an attorney first must know and understand the laws that impact settlement. There are important federal laws that can impact a client's eligibility for public benefits post settlement that must be explained. There are also financial options provided for under the Internal Revenue Code that should be explored. These issues are laid out in more detail

---

39 While most often we deal with someone who has a disability, Social Security Disability also provides death benefits. Additionally, a child who became disabled before age twenty-two and has remained continuously disabled since age eighteen may receive disability benefits based on the work history of a disabled, deceased, or retired parent as long as the child is disabled and unmarried.

40 SSDI beneficiaries receive Part A Medicare benefits, which covers inpatient hospital services, home health, and hospice benefits. Part B benefits cover physician's charges, and SSDI beneficiaries may obtain coverage by paying a monthly premium. Part D provides coverage for most prescription drugs, but it is a complicated system with a large copay called the donut hole.

with a focus on the ethical and malpractice issues raised in discussing the form of a personal injury settlement.

PUBLIC ASSISTANCE

THE MEDICARE SECONDARY PAYER ACT: §1862(B) OF THE SOCIAL SECURITY ACT

A client who is a current Medicare beneficiary or reasonably expected to become one within thirty months should concern every trial lawyer because of the implications of the Medicare Secondary Payer Act (MSP). The MSP is a series of statutory provisions[41] enacted in 1980 as part of the Omnibus Reconciliation Act[42] with the goal of reducing federal healthcare costs. The MSP provides that if a primary payer exists, Medicare pays only for medical treatment relating to an injury to the extent that the primary payer does not pay.[43] The regulations that implement the MSP provide "[s]ection 1862(b)(2)(A)(ii) of the Act precludes Medicare payments for services to the extent that payment has been made or can reasonably be expected to be made promptly under any of the following" (i) Workers' compensation; (ii) Liability insurance; (iii) No-fault insurance."[44]

There are two issues that arise when dealing with the application of the MSP: 1) Medicare payments made prior to the date of settlement (conditional payments); and 2) future Medicare payments for covered services (Medicare Set-Asides). Since Medicare isn't supposed to pay for future medical expenses covered by a liability or a workers' compensation settlement, or a judgment or

---

41   The provisions of the MSP can be found at Section 1862(b) of the Social Security Act. 42 U.S.C. § 1395y(b)(6) (2007).

42   Omnibus Reconciliation Act of 1980, Pub. L. No. 96-499 (Dec. 5, 1980).

43   42 CFR § 411.20(2) Part 411, Subpart B, (2007).

44   *Id.*

award, Centers for Medicare & Medicaid Services (CMS) recommends that injury victims set aside a sufficient amount to cover future medical expenses that are Medicare covered. CMS' recommended way to protect an injury victim's future Medicare benefit eligibility is establishment of a Medicare Set-Aside (MSA) to pay for injury-related care until exhaustion.

In certain cases, a Medicare Set-Aside may be advisable in order to preserve future eligibility for Medicare coverage. A Medicare Set-Aside allows an injury victim to preserve Medicare benefits by setting aside a portion of the settlement money in a segregated account to pay for future Medicare-covered healthcare. The funds in the Set-Aside can only be used for Medicare-covered expenses for the client's injury-related care. Once the Set-Aside account is exhausted, the client gets full Medicare coverage without Medicare looking to their remaining settlement dollars to provide for any Medicare-covered healthcare. In certain circumstances, Medicare approves the amount to be set aside in writing and agrees to be responsible for all future expenses once the Set-Aside funds are depleted.

The problem is that MSAs are not required by a federal statute even in workers' compensation cases where they are commonplace. There are no regulations, at this time, related to MSAs either. Instead, CMS has intricate "guidelines" and "FAQs" on their website for nearly every aspect of Set-Asides from submission to administration. There are only limited guidelines for liability settlements involving Medicare beneficiaries. Without codification of Set-Asides, there are no clear-cut appellate procedures from arbitrary CMS decisions and no definitive rules one can count on as it relates to Medicare Set-Asides. While there is no legal requirement that an MSA be created, the failure to do so may result in Medicare refusing to pay for future medical expenses related to the injury until the entire settlement is exhausted. There has been a slow progression toward a CMS policy of creating Set-Asides in liability settlements over the last seven years as a result of the Medicare Medicaid SCHIP Extension Act's passage.[45] This creates a difficult situation for Medicare beneficiary-injury victims and contingent liability for legal practitioners as well as other parties involved in litigation involving physical injuries to Medicare beneficiaries given the uncertainty surrounding the need to create a Set-Aside. There appears to be regulations on the horizon for Set-Asides based upon a Notice of Proposed Rulemaking from CMS entitled "Medicare Secondary Payer and Future Medicals."[46]

SPECIAL NEEDS TRUSTS: 42 U.S.C. §1396P(D)(4)

The receipt of personal injury proceeds by someone seriously injured can cause ineligibility for means-based-tested government benefit programs. Medicaid[47] and SSI[48] are two such programs. However, there are planning devices that can be utilized to preserve eligibility for disabled injury victims. An

---

45 The MMSEA created a mandatory insurer reporting requirement which tasks defendants/insurers with reporting settlements involving Medicare beneficiaries to Medicare. The reporting requirement requires settlements of $2,000 or greater to be reported as of 10/1/13. Medicare, Medicaid, and SCHIP Extension Act of 2007 (P.L. 110-173). This Act was passed by the House on December 19, 2007, and by a voice vote in the Senate on December 18, 2007.

46 See OMB Website at http://www.reginfo.gov/public/do/eAgendaViewRule?pubId=201304&RIN=0938-AR43&utm_source=hs_email&utm_medium=email&utm_content=9802088&_hsenc=p2ANqtz-_euy lttJVQH6n2LezrHHgA7PMzVcdcZQAsDlnCG1ebSm8BHxtM5Ar222rNo moh-yQJo5y49aJC-7LqU-KfmwSRwyL2xmKNhbg9vTUcuUjT1mNfif4&_hsmi=9802088.

47 Medicaid is a needs-based public benefit that provides basic healthcare coverage for those who are financially eligible. The Medicaid program is federally and state funded but administered on the state level. Services and eligibility requirements vary from state to state. The asset limit is $2,000 for most Medicaid programs but the income limits vary by state.

48 SSI or Supplemental Security Income, administered by the Social Security Administration, provides financial assistance to US citizens who are sixty-five or older, blind, or disabled. The recipient must also meet the financial eligibility requirements. 42 U.S.C. § 1382 (2007).

SNT can be created to hold the recovery and preserve public benefit eligibility, since assets held within a Special Needs Trust are not countable resources for purposes of Medicaid or SSI eligibility. The creation of Special Needs Trusts is authorized by the federal law.[49] Trusts commonly referred to as (d)(4)(a) Special Needs Trusts, named after the federal code section that authorizes their creation, are for those under the age of sixty-five.[50] However, another type of trust is authorized under the federal law with no age restriction and it is called a pooled trust, commonly referred to as a (d)(4)(c) trust.[51] These trusts are described fully below.

A personal injury recovery can be placed into a SNT so that the victim can continue to qualify for SSI and Medicaid. Federal law authorizes and regulates the creation of a SNT. The 1396p[52] provisions in the United States code govern the creation and requirements for such trusts. First and foremost, a client must be disabled in order to create a SNT.[53] There are three primary types of trusts that may be created to hold a personal injury recovery, each with its own requirements and restrictions. First is the (d)

---

49   42 U.S.C. § 1396p (d)(4) (2007).

50   42 U.S.C. § 1396p (d)(4)(A) (2007).

51   42 U.S.C. § 1396p (d)(4)(C) (2007).

52   42 U.S.C. § 1396p (2007).

53   To be considered disabled for purposes of creating an SNT, the SNT beneficiary must meet the definition of disability for SSDI found at 42 U.S.C. § 1382c. 42 U.S.C. § 1382(c)(a)(3) states that "[A]n individual shall be considered to be disabled for purposes of this title...if he is unable to engage in any substantial gainful activity by reason of any medically determinable physical or mental impairment which can be expected to result in death or...last for a continuous period of not less than twelve months (or in the case of a child under the age of 18, if that individual has a medically determinable physical or mental impairment, which results in marked and severe functional limitations, and which can be expected to result in death or...last for a continuous period of not less than twelve months)."

(4)(A)[54] Special Needs Trust which can be established only for those who are disabled and are under age sixty-five. This trust is established with the personal injury victim's recovery and is established for the victim's own benefit. It can only be established by a parent, grandparent, guardian, or court order. The injury victim can't create it on his or her own. Second is a (d)(4)(C)[55] trust, typically called a pooled trust that may be established with the disabled victim's funds regardless of age. A pooled trust can be established by the injury victim unlike a (d)(4)(A). Third and last is a third-party[56] SNT, which is funded and established by someone other than the personal injury victim (i.e., parent, grandparent, charity, etc.) for the benefit of the personal injury victim. The victim still must meet the definition of disability.

DUAL ELIGIBILITY: THE INTERSECTION OF MEDICARE AND MEDICAID— SNT/MSA

If you have a client who is a Medicaid and Medicare recipient, extra planning may be in order. If it is determined that a Medicare Set-Aside is appropriate, it raises some issues with continued

54 42 U.S.C. § 1396p (d)(4)(A) provides that a trust's assets are not countable if it is "[a] trust containing the assets of an individual under age 65 who is disabled (as defined in section 1382c(a)(3) of this title) and which is established for the benefit of such individual by a parent, grandparent, legal guardian of the individual, or a court if the State will receive all amounts remaining in the trust upon the death of such individual up to an amount equal to the total medical assistance paid on behalf of the individual under a State plan under this subchapter."

55 42 U.S.C. § 1396p (d)(4)(C) provides that a trust's assets are not countable if it is "[a] trust containing the assets of an individual who is disabled (as defined in Section 1382(a)(3) of this title) that meets the following conditions: (i) The trust is established and managed by a nonprofit association. (ii) A separate account is maintained for each beneficiary of the trust, but, for purposes of investment and management of funds, the trust pools these accounts. (iii) Accounts in the trust are established solely for the benefit of individuals who are disabled (by the parent, grandparent, or legal guardian of such individuals, by such individuals, or by a court. (iv) To the extent that amounts remaining in the beneficiary's account upon the death of the beneficiary are not retained by the trust, the trust pays to the State from such remaining amounts in the account an amount equal to the total amount of medical assistance paid on behalf of the beneficiary under the State plan under this subchapter."

56 Third-party Special Needs Trusts are creatures of the common law. Federal law does not provide requirements or regulations for these trusts.

Medicaid eligibility. A Medicare Set-Aside account is considered an available resource for purposes of needs-based benefits such as SSI/Medicaid. If the Medicare Set-Aside account is not set up inside a SNT, the client will lose Medicaid/SSI eligibility. Therefore, in order for someone with dual eligibility to maintain their Medicaid/SSI benefits, the MSA must be put inside a Special Needs Trust. In this instance, you would have a hybrid trust, which addresses both Medicaid and Medicare. It is a complicated planning tool but one that is essential when you have a client with dual eligibility.

FINANCIAL CONSIDERATIONS
PERIODIC PAYMENTS: §104(A)(2) OF THE INTERNAL REVENUE CODE

When any physical injury victim recovers money either by settlement or by verdict, the question of the tax treatment of said recovery arises. As long as it is compensation for personal physical injuries it is tax-free under Section 104(a)(2) of the Internal Revenue Code.[57] Section 104(a)(2) of the Internal Revenue Code states that "gross income does not include...the amount of any damages received (whether by suit or agreement and whether as lump sums or as periodic payments) on account of personal injuries or sickness."[58] Section 104(a)(2) gives the personal injury victim two different financial options for their recovery—lump sum or periodic payments.[59]

The first option is to take all of the personal injury recovery in a single lump sum. If this option is selected, the lump sum is not taxable, but once invested, the gains become taxable

---

57 I.R.C. § 104(a)(2) (2007).

58 Id.

59 Id.

and the receipt of the money will impact his or her ability to receive public assistance.[60] A lump sum recovery does not provide any spendthrift protection and leaves the recovery at risk for creditor claims, judgments, and potential rapid dissipation.[61] The personal injury victim has the burden of managing the money to provide for their future needs, be it wage loss or future medical. The second option is receiving "periodic payments" known as a structured settlement[62] instead of a single lump sum payment. A structured settlement's investment gains are never taxed,[63] it offers spendthrift protection,[64] and the money has enhanced protection against creditor claims as well as judgments.[65] A structured settlement recipient can avoid disqualification from public assistance when a structured settlement is used in conjunction with the appropriate public benefit preservation trust.

---

60 *Id.*

61 Unlike a structured settlement, simply receiving a lump sum does not provide any spendthrift protection as the money can be dissipated rapidly. Similarly, there is no protection from creditor claims like a structured settlement enjoys.

62 A structured settlement is a single premium fixed annuity used to provide future periodic payments to personal physical injury victims. The interest earned is not taxable under Section 104(a)(2) and a series of revenue rulings that provide the basis for structured settlements.

63 *See* I.R.C. § 104(a)(2) (2007). *See also* Rev. Rul. 79-220 (1979) (holding recipient may exclude the full amount of the single premium annuity payments received as part of a personal injury settlement from gross income under section 104(a)(2) of the code).

64 Structured settlements can't be accelerated, deferred, anticipated, or encumbered. The payments are made pursuant to the terms of the contract with the life insurance company. Thus, a personal injury victim is protected from spending the money too quickly. However, there are "factoring" companies that will purchase structured settlement annuities and provide a lump sum payment. These transactions are now regulated by IRC 5891 and many states have enacted provisions to protect structured settlement recipients from unfair transactions. IRC 5891 requires a finding that the sale is in the best interest of the annuitant and requires judicial approval.

65 Many states offer protection by statute for annuities. For example, in Florida, the Florida statutes provide annuities immunity from legal process as long as they are not set up to defraud creditors. *See generally* § 222.14 Fla. Stat. (2007).

If a structured settlement is to be used for someone eligible for needs-based public benefits such as Medicaid and/or SSI, it is vitally important that a plan be properly constructed to avoid disqualification. A structured settlement alone will never preserve public benefit eligibility and may in fact cause permanent disqualification when lifetime benefits are involved. For example, in *Sams v. DPW*, [66] a Pennsylvania court found that the purchase of a structured settlement as part of a personal injury settlement was a transfer of assets for less than fair market value, causing disqualification from needs-based benefits for the recipient. To avoid this sort of outcome, it is necessary that a structured settlement's payments be irrevocably assigned to a properly created Special Needs Trust. According to a 2006 Social Security Administration letter, "if the beneficiary of a trust which is not a resource for SSI has no right to anticipate, sell or transfer the annuity payments, the payments from a structured settlement annuity that are irrevocably assigned to an SNT, are not income to the trust beneficiary when paid into the trust."[67] In addition, under the *Sams* decision, payments should immediately start going into the trust. They cannot be deferred, and the death beneficiary of future payments should be the Special Needs Trust so as not to frustrate federal payback requirements.

---

66 *Sams v. Department of Public Welfare*, 2013 Pa. Commw. LEXIS 337 (August 21, 2013).

67 Letter from Nancy Veillon, Associate Commissioner for Income Security Programs to Roger M. Bernstein dated January 1, 2006.

CHAPTER 3

PROTECTING THE RECOVERY

ADDRESSING FINANCIAL CONSIDERATIONS WITH FUTURE PERIODIC PAYMENTS FROM STRUCTURED SETTLEMENTS

Given the obligations for personal injury practitioners to advise injury victims about the form of their financial recovery outlined in chapter 1, greater detail about the protections afforded by structured settlements is appropriate. Structured settlements utilizing life insurance annuities as their funding mechanism have been around for four decades. Over half a million injury victims receive benefits from structured settlement annuities. Each year, life insurance companies that provide structured settlements receive more than $6 billion to fund new structured settlement arrangements and an estimated $156 billion has been paid in total to fund structured settlements in force since the seventies.[68] Since 1976, in excess of 880,000 cases were settled using a structured settlement for all or part of the settlement with an average annuity premium of just over $177,000.[69]

---

68 Daniel W. Hindert & Craig H. Ulman, *Transfers of Structured Settlement Payment Rights: What Judges Should Know About Structured Settlement Protection Acts*, 44 NO. 2 Judges' J. 19 (2005); *see also* https://s2kmblog.typepad.com/rethinking_structured_set/2017/02/structured-settlement-2016-annuity-sales.html.

69 https://s2kmblog.typepad.com/rethinking_structured_set/2017/02/structured-settlement-2016-annuity-sales.html.

Structured settlements are utilized in the settlement of tort claims because of the advantages they offer like income tax-free payments,[70] fixed, low-risk competitive returns, guaranteed lifetime income, no-cost financial management, spendthrift protection, creditor protection, and avoidance of guardianship requirements in certain cases. Structured settlements offer the unsophisticated investor the ability to make a one-time, simple investment decision that will provide competitive returns with no market risk and no taxation.[71] Similarly, for sophisticated investors they can use the annuity as a funding mechanism for other investments using a dollar cost averaging approach.[72] For the injury victim, a low-risk, fixed and income-tax-free vehicle that can provide guaranteed income is very attractive and appropriate. In addition, a structured settlement can be a tool to pass wealth on to the next generation avoiding income tax on any of the income generated.[73]

GOVERNMENT OVERSIGHT OF LIFE INSURANCE COMPANIES

There are a variety of legal protections offered by structured settlements. A particularly important set of legal protections will be explored in the following paragraphs. First, annuities in general have some significant protections against loss due to insolvency of the life insurance company (the only way to lose money with a fixed annuity). There are several layers of protection against insolvency or in case of insolvency. The first layer of protection

70 *See* I.R.C. §104(a) (2008). *See also* Rev. Rul. 79-220 (July 1979) (payments are income tax-free to injury victim and all subsequent payees).

71 Richard B. Risk, Jr., *Structured Settlements: The Ongoing Evolution from a Liability Insurer's Ploy to an Injury Victim's Boon*, 36 Tulsa L. J. 865 (2001).

72 *Id.*

73 While structured settlements are income tax free even to subsequent payees, they are not estate tax free. The present value of the remaining guaranteed payments is includable in the injury victim's gross estate.

is that annuity providers are overseen by state insurance commissions. The second layer of protection is that state law imposes reserve and surplus requirements on life insurance companies. The third layer of protection is that every state has a state guaranty association which guarantees annuities. The final layer of protection is careful selection of the highest-quality annuity providers to provide structured settlements.

Life insurance companies are regulated by their domicile state's department of insurance. All the state departments of insurance are part of the National Association of Insurance Commissioners (NAIC). The NAIC is a voluntary organization comprised of the chief insurance regulatory officials of the fifty states, the District of Columbia, and the five US territories. According to the NAIC, its "overriding objective is to assist state insurance regulators in protecting consumers and helping maintain the financial stability of the insurance industry."[74] The NAIC issued a statement after the recent financial difficulties AIG experienced which stated the following:

> "As a holding company, AIG is a separate, federally regulated legal entity that is distinct and apart from its subsidiary insurers. The subsidiary insurers are governed by state laws designed to protect the interest of policyholders. State insurance regulators are committed to protecting the interest of policyholders and will work closely with AIG management and other regulators to fulfill this commitment.
>
> The No. 1 job of state insurance regulators is to make sure insurance companies operate on a financially sound basis. If needed, we immediately step in if it appears that an insurer

---

74   NAIC News Release, *Insurance Consumers Protected by Solvency Standards* (Sept. 16, 2008).

will be unable to fulfill the promises made to its policyholders. This includes taking over the management of an insurer through a conservation or rehabilitation order, the goal being to get the insurer back into a strong solvency position.

State regulators have numerous actions they can take to prevent an insurer from failing. Claims from individual policyholders are given the utmost priority over other creditors in these matters—and, in the unlikely event the assets are not enough to cover these claims, there is still another safety net in place to protect consumers: the state guaranty funds. These funds are in place in all states. If an insurance company becomes unable to pay claims, the guaranty fund will provide coverage, subject to certain limits."[75]

As the NAIC pointed out in the foregoing statement, state insurance regulators make sure insurance companies operate on a "financially sound basis." State regulation of insurance companies is the first and primary line of defense against actions by life insurance companies which potentially could lead to insolvency.

In addition to oversight by insurance commissioners and state departments of insurance, state laws require life insurance companies to maintain reserves for every obligation they undertake and regulate the types of investments a life insurance company can make. According to the National Structured Settlement Trade Association (NSSTA), "more than two-thirds of the investments corresponding to a life insurer's required reserves are held in 'investment grade' bonds, with less than five percent in the stock market." On top of reserves, life insurance companies must maintain a surplus of additional funds to meet their future

---

75   *Id.*

obligations. There are certain asset-to-liability ratios that are considered healthy. NSSTA points out that the "American Council of Life Insurers, in a recent survey, their members' average surplus ratio actually stood at a factor of over four" while assets of two and a half times liabilities are considered healthy.

State guaranty funds offer a significant line of protection to those that have annuities. According to the National Organization of Life and Health Insurance Guaranty Associations (NOLHGA), state life and health guaranty associations are state entities instituted to protect insurance policyholders from insolvent insurance companies. There is a state guaranty association in all fifty states as well as Puerto Rico and the District of Columbia. NOLHGA explains that "[t]he guaranty association cooperates with the commissioner and the receiver in determining whether the company can be rehabilitated or if the failed company should be liquidated and its policies transferred to financially sound insurance companies." Once a "liquidation is ordered, the guaranty association provides coverage to the company's policyholders who are state residents up to the limits specified by state laws."[76]

Obviously care and thought should be given for how to construct a structured settlement plan for an injury victim. Diversification and creating overlapping income streams with different companies may be advisable depending on the circumstances. Careful analysis regarding the financial strength of the life insurance companies proposed for an injury victim is also of paramount importance. There are several rating services that evaluate the strength of life insurance companies that offer structured set-

---

76 According to NOLHGA, "when an insurer fails and there is a shortfall of funds needed to meet the obligations to policyholders, state guaranty associations are activated. To amass the funds needed to protect the state's policyholders, insurers doing business in that state are assessed a share of the amount required to meet all covered claims. The amount insurers are assessed is based on the amount of premiums that they collect in that state."

tlements. The primary rating service is A.M. Best, and their top rating is A++. The other important rating service is S&P whose top rating is AAA. While companies rated A+ by A.M. Best or AA by S&P are still excellent companies, depending on risk tolerance of the client and concerns about security, a client might want to go with a company that is A++ and AAA rated. Another option for greater security is diversification whereby multiple top-rated companies are utilized instead of just one highly rated company.

As part of the ratings' analysis process, consideration should also be given to the types of investments that a life insurance company makes with its assets. For example, New York Life (rated A++ by A.M. Best and AAA by S&P) has a total of $104 billion invested assets. Bonds make up the largest percentage of their invested assets at 63.6 percent (of that 69.5 percent were class 1 highest-quality bonds and 23.9 percent were class 2 higher-quality bonds). Mortgages make up a rather small percentage of their invested assets at 8.7 percent (however 0.0 percent were classified as "problem mortgages"). In addition, there is a ratio of assets-to-liabilities measurement that is also important to consider in these turbulent financial times. New York Life's ratio is very high, meaning they are very well capitalized, as one would expect given their financial ratings.

STATE STRUCTURED SETTLEMENT PROTECTION ACTS

In addition to the foregoing legal protections, there are state structured settlement protection acts. After the advent of the "factoring" industry in the early 1990s, nearly every state has passed a structured settlement protection act. The acts protect structured settlement recipients from unscrupulous companies that purchase structured settlements. "Factoring" companies, the name commonly used for companies that purchase structured settlements, buy injury victim's payment streams in return for a lump sum payment to the injury victim. The lump sum payment to the injury victim for their future periodic structured settlement annuity payments is typically at a sharp discount with some discount rates being patently unfair.[77] Given the unsophisticated population selling structured settlements, the amount of advertising by factoring companies and past abuses by factoring companies, many states have enacted Structured Settlement Protection Acts and the federal government decided to enact protective legislation in the form of Section 5891[78] of the Internal Revenue Code.

Section 5891 of the Internal Revenue Code requires that all structured settlement factoring transactions be approved by a state court, in accordance with a qualified state statute. Qualified state statutes must make certain baseline findings, including that the transfer is in the best interest of the seller, taking into account the welfare and support of any dependents. Failure to comply with these procedures results in the factoring company paying a punitive excise tax of 40 percent on the difference between the value of the future payments sold and the amount paid to the person who wanted to sell.

State legislatures began enacting protective legislation, called Structured Settlement Protection Acts, for structured settlements in 1997.[79] While the state structured settlement protection

77   See *J.G. Wentworth S.S.C. v. Jones, Jefferson Cty.*, S.W.3d 309, 315 (Ky. Ct. App. 2000) ("[i]n the four cases here the rate of return to Wentworth varied between 36 and 68 percent per year"); *Windsor-Thomas Group Inc. v. Parker*, 782 So.2d 478 (Fla. 2d DCA 2001) (finding that from "a functional viewpoint, this agreement is a secured promissory note with an annual interest rate of approximately 100 percent.").

78   I.R.C. §5891 (2008).

79   Illinois was the first state to enact a structured settlement protection act. Hindert & Ulman, Transfers of Structured Settlement Payment Rights: What Judges Should Know About Structured Settlement Protection Acts, 44 NO. 2 Judges' J. 19 (2005).

acts vary, they are based on a model act and most contain similar provisions. While all of the acts mandate court approval of any proposed sale with a best interests' finding, most impose numerous procedural requirements and call for full disclosure of the terms of the transaction. A New York case denied a petition for approval of a "factoring" transaction under the state's structured settlement protection act because of the unfair nature of the deal, lack of a plan for the lump sum to be received, and because it was not demonstrated to serve the payee's best interests.[80] Judge Alice Schlesinger explained, in denying the approval of the sale, that "[t]he Act, similar to others nationwide, was designed 'to protect the recipients of long-term structured settlements from being victimized by companies aggressively seeking the acquisition of their rights.'"

Other courts that have interpreted the various state acts have found that they are "designed to protect beneficiaries of structured settlements from being taken advantage of by others."[81] The best interests' standard was described by a Pennsylvania court as admitting "the reality that a person's judgment is often clouded by the lure of quick cash; and insures that the public policy considerations involving structured settlements are not usurped by organizations that lure people into assigning future payments for far less than their actual value."[82]

Similarly, cases have held the structured settlement payment acts prevent garnishment of a structured settlement annuity. In

---

80 *Petition of 321 Henderson Receivables, L.P. V. Martinez*, 816 N.Y.S.2d 298 (2006) (holding "proposed sale of payee's structured settlement payments was not fair and reasonable and did not serve best interest of payee, and thus could not be approved pursuant to Structured Settlement Protection Act").

81 *In re Benninger*, 357 B.R. 337 (Bankr. WD. Pa. 2006).

82 *In re Hilton*, No. 2005-2721, 2005 WL 4171289, 2005 Pa. Dist. & Cnty. Dec. LEXIS 392 (2005).

a Pennsylvania case, the court held that a creditor's alleged security interest and garnishment of a structured settlement annuity violated the state's Structured Settlement Protection Act.[83] In interpreting the Pennsylvania Structured Settlement Protection Act, the court determined that garnishment was encompassed by the broad meaning of the word "transfer" in the act.

Another important note relates to anti-assignment provisions found in many structured settlement agreements. Most settlement releases of tort claims where a structured settlement will be implemented contain an anti-assignment provision. This provision typically states that "the periodic payments cannot be accelerated, deferred, increased, or decreased by claimant or any payee; nor shall claimant or any payee have the power to sell, mortgage, encumber, or anticipate the periodic payments, or any part thereof, by assignment or otherwise." Most state courts have held that the common law and contract rights relating to these provisions are not superseded by enactment of Structured Settlement Protection Acts.[84] Accordingly, courts have blocked the sale of structured settlements even though they complied with the state act because it would be barred by the anti-assignment clause found in the settlement documents.[85] There is model language that can be inserted into a settlement agreement that would allow for factoring, if desired, but requiring

---

83 *In re Benninger*, 357 B.R. 337 (Bankr. WD. Pa. 2006).

84 *See generally Rapid Settlements, Ltd. v. Dickerson*, 941 So.2d 1275 (Fla 4th DCA 2006) (holding assignment of payments was prohibited under settlement agreement); *Bobbitt v. Safeco Assigned Benefits Service Co.*, 25 Conn. L. Rptr. 324, 41 U.C.C. Rep. Serv. 2d 942 (Conn. Super. Ct. 1999) (holding Structured Settlement Protection Act did not abrogate the anti-assignment provision in the release and enforcing anti-assignment provision); *In re Foreman*, 365 Ill. App. 3d 608, 302 Ill. Dec. 950, 850 N.E.2d 387 (2d Dist. 2006) (rejecting a petition by factoring company under the Illinois Structured Settlement Protection Act for court approval of factoring transaction and holding anti-assignment provision in release prohibited transaction).

85 *Id.*

it comply with IRC 5891 and relevant state structured settlement protection acts.[86]

Most states impose fines and provide civil remedies for failure to comply with the state structured settlement protection act. Some deem a violation of the statute as a violation of the Unfair Trade Practices and Consumer Protection Law.[87] In addition, there is the 40 percent excise tax imposed by IRC 5891 for failure to comply with the state structured settlement protection act.[88]

The structured settlement protection acts provide significant protections for structured settlement recipients against factoring transactions and have in some instances prevented the sale of a structured settlement completely. These laws provide an additional protection for structured settlement recipients and illustrate the government's recognition of their value to injury victims.

PROTECTION FROM CREDITORS, BANKRUPTCY, AND DIVORCE

Oftentimes the protection that structured settlement annuities

---

86 Suggested model language is as follows: "None of the Periodic Payments and no rights to or interest in any of the Periodic Payments (all of the foregoing being hereinafter collectively referred to as 'Payment Rights') can be accelerated, deferred, increased or decreased by any recipient of any of the Periodic Payments; or sold, assigned, pledged, hypothecated or otherwise transferred or encumbered, either directly or indirectly, unless such sale, assignment, pledge, hypothecation or other transfer or encumbrance (any such transaction being hereinafter referred to as a 'Transfer') has been approved in advance in a 'Qualified Order' as defined in Section 5891(b)(2) of the Code (a 'Qualified Order') and otherwise complies with applicable state law, including without limitation any applicable state structured settlement protection statute. No Claimant or Successor Payee shall have the power to effect any Transfer of Payment Rights except as provided in sub-paragraph (ii) above, and any other purported Transfer of Payment Rights shall be wholly void. If Payment Rights under this Agreement become the subject of a Transfer approved in accordance with sub-paragraph (ii) above the rights of any direct or indirect transferee of such Transfer shall be subject to the terms of this Agreement and any defense or claim in recoupment arising hereunder."

87 See 40 P.S. § 4007 (P.A. 2000).

88 I.R.C. §5891 (2008).

are afforded under the law in terms of judgments and creditor claims is overlooked when analyzing whether to implement one. However, this feature is very important for injury victims who need to protect their recovery. Injury victims only get one opportunity to recover compensation for their injuries. If someone who recovers compensation for their injuries is subsequently involved in an accident where they injure someone else or someone is injured on their property, bank accounts and most investments are exposed to claims. In addition, if an injury victim gets into debt and has creditors making claims, their assets could be exposed to these claims.

However, many states have either common law or statutes that protect annuities from legal process. For example, in Florida there is a statute[89] that completely exempts annuities from creditors and judgments. This statute gives injury victims an option to completely protect their settlement proceeds from judgments or creditor claims by entering into a structured settlement annuity as part of their settlement. That statute has been interpreted by Florida courts[90] to defeat judgment creditor claims against structured settlement annuities.

In addition, structured settlements offer enhanced protection under the law in case of divorce or bankruptcy. Structured set-

---

89 §222.14, Fla. Stat. (2008). Section 222.14 provides: The cash surrender values of life insurance policies issued upon the lives of citizens or residents of the state and the proceeds of annuity contracts issued to citizens or residents of the state, upon whatever form, shall not in any case be liable to attachment, garnishment or legal process in favor of any creditor of the person whose life is so insured or of any creditor of the person who is the beneficiary of such annuity contract, unless the insurance policy or annuity contract was effected for the benefit of such creditor.

90 See Windsor-Thomas Group Inc. v. Parker, 782 So.2d 478 (Fla. 2d DCA 2001). Judgment creditor brought action to garnish annuity that funded structured settlement of tort case in favor of the judgment debtor. The issuer moved to quash the writ based on the statutory prohibition that annuity contracts are not liable to attachment, garnishment, or legal process in favor of any creditor. The Circuit Court dissolved the writ. Creditor appealed. The District Court of Appeals held that the issuer had standing to raise the statutory prohibition against garnishment.

tlements are not owned by the injury victim. Instead, the injury victim is the payee and the life insurance company's assignment company owns the annuity. When a structured settlement is created as part of a settlement, an assignment is done. The assignment is done to transfer ownership of the annuity from the purchaser (the defendant) to the life insurance company assignment corporation. The assignment corporation takes on the obligation to make the future periodic payments and purchases an annuity from the annuity issuer. Because of this legal arrangement, structured settlement annuities are not an asset owned by an injury victim. Consequently, it is not an asset that can generally be divided in the case of divorce.[91] The income that it produces can be considered in determining alimony, but the asset itself usually is not divided.[92] Similarly, a structured settlement annuity is not an asset generally reachable in cases of bankruptcy.[93]

In conclusion, structured settlements are an important planning tool for injury victims. Because of their security, tax-free return, and general shield against creditors, they should be considered as part of a comprehensive settlement plan. Because of the strong financial oversight of life insurance companies by the state departments of insurance, structured settlements are very safe and secure investment vehicles for injury victims. As such,

---

91 *See generally Krebs v. Krebs*, 435 N.W.2d 240 (Wis. 1989).

92 *See generally Ihlenfeldt v.* Ihlenfeldt, 549 N.W.2d 791 (Wis. App. 1996).

93 *See In re McCollam*, 612 So.2d 572 (Fla. 1993). Annuity was exempt under Florida statute 222.14 from creditor claims in bankruptcy action. *See also In re Orso*, 283 F.3d 686 (5th Cir. 2002) (holding structured settlement "annuity contracts under which payments were owed came within scope of Louisiana statute exempting such contracts from the claims of creditors"); *In re Belue*, 238 B.R. 218 (S.D. Fla. 1999) (holding "debtor who was named, as payee and intended beneficiary, under annuity purchased by insurance company to fund its obligations under structured settlement agreement was entitled to claim annuity payments as exempt under special Florida exemption for proceeds of any annuity contracts issued to citizens or residents of state..."); *In re Alexander*, 227 B.R. 658 (N.D. TX 1998) (holding structured settlement annuity paid to debtors following the death of their children in automobile accident was entitled to exemption as an annuity under Texas law).

having a structured settlement as the cornerstone of a financial settlement plan, can mean the difference between outliving the settlement or not.

CHAPTER 4

PROTECTING THE RECOVERY

PRESERVATION OF NEEDS-BASED BENEFITS

As discussed in chapter 2, Medicaid and SSI are income- and asset-sensitive public benefits, which require planning to preserve. In many states, one dollar of SSI benefits automatically provides Medicaid coverage. A Special Needs Trust is a trust that can be created pursuant to federal law whose corpus or any assets held in the trust do not count as resources for purposes of qualifying for Medicaid or SSI. Thus, a personal injury recovery can be placed into a SNT so that the victim can continue to qualify for SSI and Medicaid. Federal law authorizes and regulates the creation of a SNT. The 1396p[94] provisions in the United States Code govern the creation and requirements for such trusts. First and foremost, a client must be disabled in order to create a SNT.[95] There are three primary types of trusts that may be cre-

---

94   42 U.S.C. § 1396p.

95   To be considered disabled for purposes of creating an SNT, the SNT beneficiary must meet the definition of disability for SSDI found at 42 U.S.C. § 1382c. 42 U.S.C. § 1382(c)(a)(3) states that "[A] n individual shall be considered to be disabled for purposes of this title...if he is unable to engage in any substantial gainful activity by reason of any medically determinable physical or mental impairment which can be expected to result in death or...last for a continuous period of not less than twelve months (or in the case of a child under the age of 18, if that individual has a medically determinable physical or mental impairment, which results in marked and severe functional limitations, and which can be expected to result in death or...last for a continuous period of not less than 12 months)."

ated to hold a personal injury recovery and one type used when it isn't the injury victim's own assets, each with its own unique requirements and restrictions. First is the (d)(4)(A)[96] Special Needs Trust, which can be established only for those who are disabled and are under age sixty-five. This trust is established with the personal injury victim's recovery and is established for the victim's own benefit. Second is a (d)(4)(C)[97] trust typically called a pooled trust that may be established with the disabled victim's funds without regard to age. The third is a trust that can be utilized if an elderly client has too much income from Social Security or a pension to qualify for some Medicaid-based nursing home assistance programs. This trust is authorized by the federal law under (d)(4)(B)[98] and is commonly referred to as a Miller Trust. Lastly, there is a third-party[99] SNT which is funded and established by someone other than the personal injury victim (i.e., parent, grandparent, donations, etc.) for the benefit of the personal injury victim. The victim still must meet the definition of disability but there is no required payback of Medicaid at death as there is with a (d)(4)(A) or (d)(4)(C).

---

96   42 U.S.C. § 1396p (d)(4)(A) provides that a trust's assets are not countable if it is "[a] trust containing the assets of an individual under age 65 who is disabled (as defined in section 1382c (a) (3) of this title) and which is established for the benefit of such individual by a parent, grandparent, legal guardian of the individual, or a court if the State will receive all amounts remaining in the trust upon the death of such individual up to an amount equal to the total medical assistance paid on behalf of the individual under a State plan under this subchapter."

97   42 U.S.C. § 1396p (d)(4)(C) provides that a trust's assets are not countable if it is "[a] trust containing the assets of an individual who is disabled (as defined in section 1382c (a)(3) of this title) that meets the following conditions: (i) The trust is established and managed by a nonprofit association. (ii) A separate account is maintained for each beneficiary of the trust, but, for purposes of investment and management of funds, the trust pools these accounts. (iii) Accounts in the trust are established solely for the benefit of individuals who are disabled (as defined in section 1382c (a)(3) of this title) by the parent, grandparent, or legal guardian of such individuals, by such individuals, or by a court. (iv) To the extent that amounts remaining in the beneficiary's account upon the death of the beneficiary are not retained by the trust, the trust pays to the State from such remaining amounts in the account an amount equal to the total amount of medical assistance paid on behalf of the beneficiary under the State plan under this subchapter."

98   42 U.S.C. § 1396p (d)(4)(B).

99   Third-party Special Needs Trusts are creatures of the common law. Federal law does not provide requirements or regulations for these trusts.

Since the pooled (d)(4)(C) trust and the (d)(4)(A) SNT are most commonly used with personal injury recoveries, it is useful to compare these two types of trusts. There are several significant differences between a (d)(4)(C) pooled trust and a (d)(4)(A) Special Needs Trust. I will discuss these differences first starting with the (d)(4)(C) pooled trust. As a starting point, a disabled injury victim joins an already established pooled trust as there is no individually crafted trust document. There are four major requirements under federal law necessary to establish a pooled trust. First, the trust must be established and managed by a non-profit.[100] Second, the trust must maintain separate accounts for each beneficiary, but the funds are pooled for purposes of investment and management.[101] Third, each trust account must be established solely for the benefit of an individual who is disabled as defined by law, and it may only be established by that individual, the individual's parent, grandparent, legal guardian, or a court.[102] Fourth, any funds that remain in a beneficiary's account at that beneficiary's death must be retained by the trust or used to reimburse the state Medicaid agency.[103]

In directly comparing a (d)(4)(C) to a (d)(4)(A) Special Needs Trust, there are four primary differences. First, a (d)(4)(A) Special Needs Trust can only be created for those under age sixty-five. However, a (d)(4)(C) pooled Special Needs Trust has no such age restriction and can be created for someone of any age. Second, a pooled Special Needs Trust is not an individually crafted trust like a (d)(4)(A) Special Needs Trust. Instead, a disabled individual joins a pooled trust and a professional nonprofit trustee

---

100 42 U.S.C. § 1396p (d)(4)(C).

101 *Id.*

102 *Id.*

103 *Id.*

pools the assets together for purposes of investment, but each beneficiary of the trust has his or her own sub-account. Third, a pooled trust is managed by a not-for-profit entity who acts as trustee overseeing distributions of the money. The nonprofit trustee may manage the money themselves or hire a separate money manager to oversee investment of the trust assets. Fourth, at death, the nonprofit trustee may retain whatever assets are left in the trust instead of repaying Medicaid for services they have provided, which is a requirement with a (d)(4)(A) Special Needs Trust.[104] By joining a pooled trust, a disabled aged injury victim can make a charitable donation to the nonprofit who manages the pooled trust and avoid the repayment requirement found within the federal law for (d)(4)(A) Special Needs Trusts. Other than the aforementioned differences, it operates as any other Special Needs Trust does, with the same restrictions on the use of the trust assets.

With a (d)(4)(A) Special Needs Trust, a trustee needs to be selected, unlike the pooled trust where it is automatically a nonprofit entity. This provides some flexibility to the family or loved ones to have a hand in the selection of the trust company or bank acting as trustee. However, it is important to have a trustee experienced in dealing with needs-based government benefit eligibility requirements so that only proper distributions are made. Many banks and trust companies don't want to administer Special Needs Trusts with a corpus under $1,000,000, which can make it difficult to find the right trustee. Most pooled Special Needs Trusts will accept any sized trust and the nonprofit is experienced in dealing with people receiving disability-based public benefits.

---

104 If the funds remaining in the trust at death are sufficient to repay Medicaid's payback right in full, many pooled trusts will distribute some portion of the remaining monies to the trust beneficiary's heirs. However, each pooled trust will have a different policy and the amount retained at death can vary greatly. It is very important to investigate how much is retained in this type of situation. Some trusts will only retain $5,000 while others may retain $50,000.

With the (d)(4)(A), there are no startup costs except the legal fee to draft the trust which can vary greatly. The (d)(4)(C) pooled trusts typically have a one-time fee at inception which can range from $500 to $2,000, which is typically much cheaper than the cost of establishing a (d)(4)(A) Special Needs Trust. Most trustees (pooled or (d)(4)(A)) will charge an ongoing annual fee, which is typically a percentage of the trust assets. These fees vary between 1–3 percent depending on how much money is in the trust. A (d)(4)(A) will offer unlimited investment choices for the funds held in the trust while a (d)(4)(C) will have fewer investment choices.

The major limitation of all types of Special Needs Trusts is that the assets held in trust can only be used for the sole benefit of the trust beneficiary. The disabled injury victim could not withdraw money and gift it to a charity or family. The purpose of the Special Needs Trust is to retain Medicaid eligibility, and use trust funds to meet the supplemental, or "special" needs of the beneficiary. These can be quite broad, however, and include things that improve health or comfort such as non-Medicaid-covered medical and dental expenses, trained medical assistance staff (twenty-four hours or as needed), independent medical checkups, medical equipment, supplies, programs of cognitive and visual training, respiratory care and rehabilitation (physical, occupational, speech, visual, and cognitive), eyeglasses, transportation (including vehicle purchase), vehicle maintenance, insurance, essential dietary needs, and private nurses or other qualified caretakers. Also included are nonmedical items, such as electronic equipment, vacations, movies, trips, travel to visit relatives or friends, and other monetary requirements to enhance the client's self-esteem, comfort, or situation. The trust may generally pay for expenses that are not "food and shelter" which are part of the SSI disability benefit payment. However, even these items could be paid for with trust assets, but SSI payments could be reduced or eliminated. This may not be problematic if the disabled injury victim qualifies for Medicaid without SSI eligibility. However, many states grant automatic Medicaid eligibility with SSI so one has to be careful about eliminating the SSI benefit.

Each type of trust discussed above has advantages and disadvantages. Some think of pooled trusts as only being appropriate for a smaller settlement, which is not the case. Some think of pooled trusts just for the elderly, which is not the case either. In the right case, the pooled trust is an excellent alternative to a (d)(4)(A). Just the same, in some cases, a (d)(4)(A) may be the best option because of the flexibility in selecting a trustee and the customizable money management options. In the end though, a Special Needs Trust, be it pooled or a (d)(4)(A), must be considered because it will safeguard a disabled client's recovery from dissipation and protect future eligibility for needs-based public benefits. Just as importantly, the different types of trusts and their advantages as well as disadvantages should be closely considered before making a decision since Special Needs Trusts are irrevocable along with bringing substantial restrictions on how the money may be used. Creating a Special Needs Trust for a disabled injury victim gives them the ability to enjoy the settlement proceeds while preserving critical healthcare coverage along with government cash assistance programs.

In conclusion, the evaluation of different methods for protecting needs-based benefit preservation must be explored for any disabled client who is currently eligible. Special needs trusts allow injury victims to continue to access critical needs-based government benefits after settling their case. Every case and client is different though and careful consideration of the advantages and disadvantages should be done with an elder law attorney.

NEEDS-BASED PUBLIC BENEFITS CASE STUDIES

To better understand how to apply the foregoing information, I will illustrate with a few case examples. First, consider a settlement for John Doe who was injured at age thirty after having worked up until the accident. Since John was a laborer since age eighteen and was still young, he didn't have health insurance at the time of his accident. As a result of being paralyzed, the hospital applied for Medicaid on his behalf after getting injured. He qualified for Medicaid, since he had no real assets and no longer had an income. His family applied for Social Security Disability, since he had worked enough quarters to be insured. You have settled his case for $1,000,000, which will help him pay for everything he now needs, but it is far less than what is needed to pay for all his future medical care. The question now is what to do with the settlement? While SSDI isn't income or asset sensitive, Medicaid is most likely the program John has, and it will have an asset cap of $2,000. In this situation, a stand-alone or pooled Special Needs Trust would be advisable to keep the Medicaid intact. SSDI alone wouldn't necessitate a Special Needs Trust.

Second, consider the case of Jane Doe who is sixty-eight. She never worked outside of the home and was recently the victim of medical malpractice. She has a private insurance policy that she can no longer pay for after becoming disabled from the stroke she suffered, which wasn't diagnosed in a timely manner. She needs to be in an assisted living facility due to the stroke. She qualified for both Medicaid and SSI after the stroke. In addition, she gets a small amount of Social Security benefits as a result of her husband's death. You have settled her case for the policy limits of the doctor who had missed the diagnosis, which is $250,000. This is completely inadequate to care for Jane. How will she qualify for nursing home care paid for by Medicaid given the small settlement? Can she keep her SSI intact? Will the death benefits cause an income problem? The solution to the first two questions is to create a pooled Special Needs Trust. As Jane is over sixty-five, she cannot create a stand-alone SNT, so her only option is a pooled trust, which will protect both her Medicaid and SSI eligibility. The SS retirement likely isn't a problem since she already has Medicaid/SSI, but if she does have an income problem, a Miller Trust or Qualified Income Trust could be established to deal with the excess income.

CHAPTER 5

MEDICAID LIEN RESOLUTION FUNDAMENTALS

In the foregoing chapter, different methods were explored to preserve eligibility for needs-based government benefits. For clients who are on Medicaid, they will most likely have a Medicaid lien when their case is settled. Every state must comply with federal Medicaid statutes and regulations to participate in the joint federal-state Medicaid program. Pursuant to Title XIX of the Social Security Act, the federal Medicaid program requires every participating state to enact a "third-party liability" provision which empowers a state to seek reimbursement from liable third parties for injury-related medical expenditures paid on behalf of a Medicaid recipient.[105] In order to comply with this requirement, a state Medicaid program must have statutory provisions under which the Medicaid recipient is considered to have assigned to the state his or her right to recover from liable third-parties' medical expenses paid by Medicaid. Federal law codifies this stating:[106]

---

105 *See* 42 U.S.C. §1396a(a)(25).

106 42 U.S.C. §1396a(a)(25)(H).

(H) that to the extent that payment has been made under the State Plan for medical assistance in any case where a third party has a legal liability to make payment for such assistance, the State has in effect laws under which, to the extent that payment has been made under the State Plan for medical assistance for healthcare items or services furnished to an individual, the State is considered to have acquired the rights of such individual to payment by any other party for such healthcare items or services.

Despite the mandate in federal law for state Medicaid agencies to seek reimbursement from liable third parties by "acquiring the rights of such individual to payment by any other party for such healthcare items or services," there are important limitations on a state's recovery rights which protect the Medicaid recipient's property. The limitation comes from the federal anti-lien statute which proclaims "[n]o lien may be imposed against the property of any individual prior to his death on account of medical assistance paid," and the federal anti-recovery statute at §1396p(b)(1) states "[n]o adjustment or recovery of any medical assistance correctly paid on behalf of an individual under the state plan may be made."[107]

The tension between these provisions in federal law and state law recovery statutes has become the source of litigation in federal as well as state courts. When these cases reached the top court in the land, the Supreme Court held that federal provisions preempt and limit a state's right to seek reimbursement from a Medicaid recipient's settlement to the extent that it reaches elements of damages beyond past medical expenses. The United States Supreme Court first weighed in on the rights of a state

---

107 42 U.S.C. §1396p(a)(1)

Medicaid agency to recover from personal injury settlements via state third-party liability recovery statutes in 2006. The Supreme Court's decision in *Arkansas Department of Health and Human Services v. Heidi Ahlborn*[108] limited a state Medicaid program's ability to assert a lien against the entire recovery from a third-party tortfeasor. The United States Supreme Court interpreted federal law authorizing states to recover Medicaid payments in a tort action to be limited to medical payments.[109] Stated a different way, the *Ahlborn* decision forbids recovery by Medicaid state agencies against the nonmedical portion of the settlement or judgment.[110] Nonmedical portions of a settlement or judgment are damages such as pain and suffering or lost wages. According to the court in *Ahlborn*:

> ...[t]here is no question that the State can require an assignment of the right, or chose in action, to receive payments for medical care. So much is expressly provided for by §§1396a(a)(25) and 1396k(a). And we assume, as do the parties, that the State can also demand as a condition of Medicaid eligibility that the recipient "assign" in advance any payments that may constitute reimbursement for medical costs. To the extent that the forced assignment is expressly authorized by the terms of §§1396a(a)(25) and 1396k(a), it is an exception to the anti-lien provision. See *Washington State Dept. of Social and Health Servs. v. Guardianship Estate of Keffeler*, 537 U. S. 371, 383–385, and n. 7 (2003). But that does not mean that the State can force an assignment of, or place a lien on, any other portion of Ahlborn's property. As explained above, the exception carved out by §§1396a(a)(25) and 1396k(a) is lim-

---

108 547 U.S. 268 (2006).

109 *See Ahlborn* 547 U.S. at 290.

110 *Id.*

ited to payments for medical care. Beyond that, the anti-lien provision applies.[111]

The holding of *Ahlborn* was a surprising result and has had a significant impact on personal injury litigation. In some instances, it has resulted in a much larger net amount being available to the injury victim at the "expense of the States' ability to recover Medicaid expenditures."[112]

When the *Ahlborn* decision was published, it was hailed by the Center for Constitutional Litigation (hereinafter "CCL"), associated with the American Trial Lawyers Association (now "American Association for Justice"), as a "significant victory" for injury victims.[113] Other commentators have agreed with the CCL that it represents a major victory for injury victims.[114] State courts have limited its application in some instances or found it wholly inapplicable.

AHLBORN BY THE FACTS

Heidi Ahlborn was injured in a very serious car accident in January of 1996.[115] At the time, she was a nineteen-year-old college student pursuing a degree in teaching.[116] She suffered a catastrophic brain injury that left her incapable of finishing college

---

111 *Id.* at 284.

112 Joseph D. Juenger, *In Light of Ahlborn—Designing State Legislation to Protect the Recovery of Medicaid Expenses from Personal Injury Settlements*, 35 N. Ky. L. Rev. 103 (2008).

113 Lou Bograd, Center for Constitutional Litigation, P.C., Memorandum to Interested Parties, *Possible Extension of Ahlborn Ruling to Medicare and Guidance to Plaintiff's Counsel Regarding the Decision* (May 16, 2006).

114 Juenger, *supra* note 6 at 103.

115 *Ahlborn*, 547 U.S. at 273.

116 *Id.*

and unable to care for or support herself in the future.[117] Due to her injuries and lack of assets, Ahlborn qualified for Medicaid coverage in Arkansas.[118] Medicaid paid Arkansas healthcare providers $215,645.30 for injury-related care on her behalf.[119]

After the accident, a personal injury action was filed on behalf of Heidi in April of 1997.[120] The damages sought included not only past medical costs but also for her "permanent physical injury; future medical expenses, past and future pain, suffering and mental anguish; past loss of earnings and working time; and permanent impairment of the ability to earn in the future."[121] During the pendency of the litigation, the Arkansas Department of Health Services (hereinafter "ADHS") sent Ahlborn's personal injury attorneys periodic notices regarding the outlays by Medicaid on behalf of Ms. Ahlborn.[122] The letters indicated that Arkansas law provided ADHS with a claim for reimbursement from "any settlement, judgment or award" that was obtained from "a third party who may be liable" for Heidi Ahlborn's injuries and no settlement "shall be satisfied without first giving [ADHS] notice and a reasonable opportunity to establish its interest."[123]

When the suit was filed, ADHS wasn't notified of the suit, as requested. Plaintiff's counsel did inform ADHS of the available

---

117 *Id.*

118 *Id.*

119 *Id.*

120 *Id.*

121 *Id.*

122 *Id.* at 274.

123 *Id.*

insurance coverage in the suit.[124] ADHS intervened in the personal injury action in February of 1998 to assert a lien against any proceeds from a settlement or judgment.[125] The case was ultimately settled in 2002 without, per customary practice, any allocation of the settlement proceeds between categories of damages.[126] ADHS asserted a lien against the settlement for the total amount of the payments made by ADHS for Ahlborn's care which totaled $215,645.30.[127]

In September of 2002, Ahlborn filed suit in the United States District Court for the Eastern District of Arkansas seeking a declaratory judgment that "the lien violated the federal Medicaid laws insofar as its satisfaction would require depletion of compensation for injuries other than past medical expenses."[128] Certain stipulations were entered into by the parties in the litigation in the US District Court. Firstly, ADHS and Ahlborn stipulated that Heidi Ahlborn's total claim "was reasonably valued at $3,040,708.18."[129] Secondly, the parties agreed that the out-of-court settlement reached represented "one-sixth of that sum."[130] Thirdly, the parties stipulated that if the plaintiff's "construction of federal law was correct, ADHS would be entitled to only the portion of the settlement ($35,581.47) that constituted reimbursement for medical payments made."[131]

---

124 *Id.*

125 *Id.*

126 *Id.*

127 *Id.*

128 *Id.*

129 *Id.*

130 *Id.*

131 *Id.*

On cross motions for summary judgment, the federal district court found that Ahlborn, under Arkansas law, assigned to ADHS her right to any tort recovery from third parties to the "full extent of Medicaid's payments for her benefit."[132] The court held accordingly that ADHS was entitled to its full lien amount of $215,645.30.[133] The ruling was appealed to the Eighth Circuit and the judgment of the District Court was reversed.[134] The Eighth Circuit held that ADHS was only entitled to the portion of the settlement attributable to payments for medical care.[135] ADHS appealed to the United States Supreme Court which affirmed the Eighth Circuit's decision.[136]

The heart of the controversy before the Supreme Court was the interpretation of federal law requiring state Medicaid programs to recover from third-party tortfeasors amounts paid on behalf of an injury victim.[137] State Medicaid agencies must "take all reasonable measures to ascertain the legal liability of third parties... to pay for care and services available under the plan."[138] Federal law also requires state Medicaid agencies to seek recovery from third parties where the reimbursement the state will receive exceeds the costs of recovery.[139] States are required to enact state statutes to facilitate recovery of such claims by providing an assignment from the injury victim to the state Medicaid agency

---

132 *Id.*

133 *Id.*

134 *Id.* at 275.

135 *Id.*

136 *Id.*

137 *Id.*

138 *Id.* (quoting 42 U.S.C. §1396a(a)(25)(A)).

139 42 U.S.C. §1396a(a)(25)(B).

for recovery of third-party medical care payments.[140] Finally, the amount collected by the state Medicaid agency "shall be retained by the State as is necessary to reimburse it for medical assistance payments made on behalf of" the Medicaid recipient.[141]

Arkansas had complied with federal law and enacted statutes providing ADHS with the right to recover "the cost of benefits" from third parties.[142] Arkansas law provided that as a "condition of eligibility," Medicaid applicants "shall automatically assign his or her right to any settlement, judgment, or award which may be obtained against any third party to [ADHS] to the full extent of any amount which may be paid by Medicaid for the benefit of the applicant."[143] Further, the Arkansas statute provided that ADHS "shall have a right to recover" when medical assistance is provided to the Medicaid recipient due to "injury, disease, or disability for which another person is liable."[144] It was pursuant to this statute that the ADHS claimed an entitlement to recover all of the costs expended on Ahlborn's behalf even though it would be recovered from portions of a settlement that didn't represent medical expenses.[145]

The question squarely before the United States Supreme Court was whether the ADHS could "lay claim to more than the portion of Ahlborn's settlement that represents medical expenses."[146] Justice Stevens said in the opinion that the "text of the federal

---

140 42 U.S.C. §1396a(a)(25)(H); *see also* 42 U.S.C. §1396k(a).

141 42 U.S.C. §1396k(a).

142 *Ahlborn* 547 U.S. at 277 (citing Ark. Code Ann. §§20-77-301 through 20-77-309 (2001)).

143 *Id.* at 277.

144 *Id.*

145 *Id.* at 278.

146 *Id.* at 280.

third-party liability provisions suggests not; it focuses on recovery of payments for medical care."[147] While the state of Arkansas made many legal arguments to the Supreme Court as to why ADHS' lien attached to Ahlborn's entire settlement, each was rejected by the court. Arkansas' primary legal argument was that the federal statute mandated every state to pass laws that require the assignment of a Medicaid beneficiary's rights to the state and assertion of liens to collect from the entire third-party recovery.[148] Justice Stevens addressed this argument by pointing to federal law which says the "State must be assigned 'the rights of [the recipient] to payment by any other part for such healthcare items or services.'"[149] According to the court, federal law didn't sanction "an assignment of rights to payment for anything other than medical expenses—not lost wages, not pain and suffering, not an inheritance."[150] This was not the basis of the court's decision in favor of Ahlborn though.

Instead, the court's decision rested on its interpretation of the "anti-lien"[151] statute in the United States Code.[152] The anti-lien statute prohibits states from exerting liens against a Medicaid recipient's property prior to death for medical assistance paid on their behalf except in specifically enumerated situations.[153] While the court found one of the anti-lien statute's enumerated exceptions was relevant to Ahlborn's situation, it was the assignment of a Medicaid beneficiary's rights to the state and assertion

147 *Id.*

148 *Id.* at 281.

149 *Id.*

150 *Id.*

151   42 U.S.C. §1396p

152   *Ahlborn,* 547 U.S. at 284.

153   *Id.*

of liens to collect from a third-party recovery which it found was limited only to medical care.[154] Accordingly, because the exception that was carved out was limited to payments for medical care, the anti-lien provision bars recovery by ADHS against the portion of Ahlborn's settlement that was nonmedical.[155]

Arkansas made several public policy arguments as to why a rule of full reimbursement was needed. The most "colorable" argument was that there was an "inherent danger of manipulation in cases where the parties to a tort case settle without judicial oversight or input from the State."[156] The court found that this issue was not before them because the ADHS had stipulated that only $35,581.47 of Ahlborn's settlement proceeds were attributable to payment for medical costs.[157] Nevertheless, Justice Stevens pointed out that "[e]ven in the absence of such a post-settlement agreement, though, the risk that parties to a tort suit will allocate away the State's interest can be avoided either by obtaining the State's advance agreement to an allocation or, if necessary by submitting the matter to a court for decision."[158] He went on to say "just as there are risks in underestimating the value of readily calculable damages in settlement negotiations, so also is there a countervailing concern that a rule of absolute priority might preclude settlement in a large number of cases, and be unfair to the recipient in others."[159]

Since the primary holding in *Ahlborn* is that federal laws that

---

154 *Id.*

155 *Id.*

156 *Id.* at 288.

157 *Id.*

158 *Id.*

159 *Id.*

authorize states to assert recoveries against third parties who have provided payments for medical care for Medicaid beneficiaries only applies to the portions of a settlement that represent compensation for past medical expenses, it appeared to invalidate state statutes that require full reimbursement of Medicaid expenditures from a third-party recovery. After the *Ahlborn* decision, states began to revise their third-party liability statutes with inconsistent results in the courts. In 2012, a challenge of the North Carolina Medicaid's third-party liability recovery statute would lead the United States Supreme Court to again weigh in on state Medicaid agencies rights to recover.

In *E.M.A. v. Cansler*,[160] the Fourth Circuit Court of Appeal agreed with the Third Circuit that in determining what portion of a Medicaid beneficiary's third-party recovery a state Medicaid agency may claim as reimbursement for Medicaid expenses, the state must have in place procedures that allow a dissatisfied beneficiary to challenge a statutory default allocation. In reaching its conclusion, the Fourth Circuit also held that the North Carolina Supreme Court wrongly interpreted *Ahlborn* in upholding the validity of North Carolina's statutory default allocation in a previous decision.

According to the *E.M.A.* decision, the United State Supreme Court's unanimous decision in *Ahlborn* makes clear, "federal Medicaid law limits a state's recovery to settlement proceeds that are shown to be properly allocable to **past** medical expenses. In the event of an unallocated lump-sum settlement exceeding the amount of the state's Medicaid expenditures, as in this case, the sum certain allocable to medical expenses must be determined by way of a fair and impartial adversarial procedure that affords

---

160 674 F.3d 290 (4th Cir. 2012), *cert. granted sub nom.* Delia v. E.M.A., 567 U.S. __ (Sept. 25, 2012).

the Medicaid beneficiary an opportunity to rebut the statutory presumption in favor of the state that allocation of one-third of a lump sum settlement is consistent with the anti-lien provision in federal law."[161]

The Fourth Circuit went on to say, "The Supreme Court has characterized the third-party liability provisions in federal Medicaid law as an exception to the anti-lien provisions, stating that "[t]o the extent that the forced assignment [of payments that constitute reimbursement for medical expenses] is expressly authorized in §§ 1396a(a)(25) and 1396k(a), it is an exception to the anti-lien provision." Ahlborn, 547 U.S. at 284, 126 S.Ct. 1752 (citing *Wash. State Dep't of Soc. & Health Servs. v. Guardianship Estate of Keffeler*, 537 U.S. 371, 383-85, & n. 7, 123 S.Ct. 1017, 154 L.Ed.2d 972 (2003)). At the same time, the Supreme Court has emphasized that this exception is strictly limited—a state cannot force assignment of, or place a lien on, any property that does not constitute reimbursement for medical expenses. *Id.* at 284-85, 126 S.Ct. 1752 ("[T]he exception carved out by §§ 1396a(a)(25) and 1396k(a) is limited to payments for medical care. Beyond that, the anti-lien provision applies.")."

The Fourth Circuit did not agree with North Carolina's argument that its statute set a "reasonable cap" on the state's recovery and therefore satisfied the federal anti-lien law.[162] Instead, the court concluded that North Carolina's one-third cap on a Medicaid recipient's settlement proceeds does not satisfy *Ahlborn* insofar as it permits North Carolina to assert a lien against settlement proceeds intended to compensate the Medicaid recipient for

---

161 *Id.* at 312 (emphasis added)

162 *Id.* at 308.

other claims, such as pain and suffering or lost wages.[163] The court declined to express a view as to whether allocation disputes must be adjudicated by a court, or may instead be resolved through other "special rules and procedures" alluded to in *Ahlborn*. However, the court held that in determining what portion of a Medicaid beneficiary's third-party recovery the state may claim in reimbursement for Medicaid expenses, it must have in place procedures that allow a dissatisfied beneficiary to challenge the default allocation.[164] As the North Carolina statute had no such provision, the court remanded the case back to the district court to make the allocation.

The United States Supreme Court granted Certiorari on September 25, 2012. Oral arguments occurred on January 8, 2013. The court rendered its opinion on March 20, 2013 upholding the Fourth Circuit's judgment in a six-to-three decision.[165] In *WOS v. EMA*, the Supreme Court was asked to review North Carolina's Medicaid Third-Party Liability Recovery statute. North Carolina's statute required that up to one-third of any damages recovered by a beneficiary for their injuries must be paid to Medicaid to reimburse it for payments it made on account of the injury. The Supreme Court found that this statute was not compatible with the federal anti-lien provision and violated the holding of *Ahlborn* which "precludes attachment or encumbrance" of any portion of a settlement not "designated as payments for medical care."[166]

The *WOS* decision discussed the tension between the mandate under federal law requiring an assignment to the state of "the

---

163 *Id.* at 307.

164 *Id.* at 311.

165 *WOS v. E.M.A.*, 133 S. CT. 1391, 185 L. Ed. 2d 471(2013).

166 *Id.*

right to recover that portion of a settlement that represents payments for medical care," and the preclusion of "attachment or encumbrance of the remainder of the settlement." The *Ahlborn* opinion held that the federal Medicaid statute sets both a floor and a ceiling on a state's potential share of a beneficiary's tort recovery. The *WOS* Court pointed out that an injury victim has a property right in the proceeds of a settlement "bringing it within the ambit of the anti-lien provision."[167] "That property right is subject to the specific statutory 'exception' requiring a State to seek reimbursement for medical expenses paid on the beneficiary's behalf, but the anti-lien provision protects the beneficiary's interest in the remainder of the settlement."[168]

North Carolina's statute as applied ran afoul of the holding in *Ahlborn* because it set "forth no process for determining what portion of a beneficiary's tort recovery is attributable to medical expenses." Instead, the statute applies an arbitrary figure (one-third) and mandates that amount be the payment for medical care out of the tort recovery. As applied, this violates the federal anti-lien law and is therefore preempted. The *WOS* Court pointed out that if "a State arbitrarily may designate one-third of any recovery as payment for medical expenses, there is no logical reason why it could not designate half, three-quarters, or all of a tort recovery in the same way."[169] Since North Carolina could provide no evidence to substantiate the claim it made that the one-third allocation was reasonable and provided no mechanism for determining whether it was a reasonable approximation in any particular case, the court rejected its application.

167 *Id.*

168 *Id.*

169 *Id.*

In a very important part of the decision, the *WOS* Court discusses when the state may not demand recovery from a portion of the settlement allocated to nonmedical damages. The court stated that when "there has been a judicial finding or approval of an allocation between medical and nonmedical damages—in the form of either a jury verdict, court decree, or stipulation binding on all parties—that is the end of the matter."[170] "With a stipulation or judgment under this procedure, the anti-lien provision protects from state demand the portion of a beneficiary's tort recovery that the stipulation or judgment does not attribute to medical expenses."[171]

In applying all of the foregoing to the facts of the case, the *WOS* Court pointed out the flaws of the North Carolina statute which didn't allow for an allocation. The court found that a substantial share of the damages in the settlement must be allocated to skilled home care in the *future*. This would not be reachable by the state Medicaid agency to satisfy their lien. In addition, the *WOS* Court noted that it may also be necessary to consider how much EMA and her parents could have expected to receive in terms of compensation for the other tort claims made in the suit had it gone to trial. "An irrebuttable, one-size-fits-all statutory presumption is incompatible with the Medicaid Act's clear mandate that a State may not demand any portion of a beneficiary's tort recovery except the share that is attributable to medical expenses."[172]

As a trial lawyer, it is important to understand the underpinnings of the *Ahlborn* and *WOS* decisions so you can apply them to your

---

170 *Id.*

171 *Id.*

172 *Id.*

state's third-party liability recovery provisions. The important thing to remember is that these cases limit a state Medicaid agency's recovery rights related to a third-party liability settlement. In order to reduce a Medicaid lien, state-specific statutes must be followed, but arguments to reduce should be based on the principles espoused in *Ahlborn* and *WOS* so that the lien is reduced in proportion to the full value of damages versus what was received.

CHAPTER 6

INTRODUCTION TO MEDICARE COMPLIANCE

Given all the complexities of the Medicare Secondary Payer Act, chapters 6 through 13 are dedicated to covering this topic in a lot of detail. While I could write an entire book just on the Medicare Secondary Payer Act, the following chapters give an overview regarding critical issues for trial lawyers to consider. Most lawyers find this area of the law very confusing at best and downright confounding at worst. The following chapters are an attempt to give a framework and guide to dealing with the most important issues when you represent a Medicare beneficiary.

The government takes its reimbursement rights seriously and is willing to pursue trial lawyers who ignore Medicare's interests. On January 8, 2020, the United States Attorney William M. McSwain announced that "a Philadelphia-based personal injury law firm...entered into a settlement agreement with the United States to resolve allegations that it failed to reimburse the United States for certain Medicare payments." As part of the settlement, like in other cases, the firm agreed to pay $6,604.59 to satisfy the debt owed to Medicare. In addition, the firm agreed to: "(1) name a person responsible for paying Medicare secondary payer debts;

(2) train the employee to ensure that the firm pays these debts on a timely basis; (3) review any additional outstanding debts to ensure compliance; and (4) provide written certifications of compliance." The firm also acknowledged that any future "failure to submit timely repayment of Medicare secondary payer debt may result in liability for the wrongful retention of a government overpayment under the False Claims Act." The following quote from McSwain sums it all up: "Lawyers need to set a good example and follow the rules of the road for Medicare reimbursement. If they don't, we will move aggressively to recover the money for taxpayers."

Last year on November 4, 2019, the United States Attorney for the District of Maryland announced that a Baltimore-based law firm paid the United States $91,406.98 to resolve allegations that it failed to pay Medicare for conditional payments that had been paid on behalf of the firm's clients. The press release indicates that the firm had entered into a joint-representation agreement with co-counsel who, in turn, didn't reimburse Medicare at settlement. According to US Attorney Robert K. Hur, "Plaintiffs' attorneys cannot refer a case to or enter into a joint-representation agreement with co-counsel and simply wash their hands clean of their obligations to reimburse Medicare for its conditional payments." He went on to say, "[w]e intend to hold attorneys accountable for failing to make good on their obligations to repay Medicare for its conditional payments, regardless of whether they were the ones primarily handling the litigation for the plaintiff." So, this is a warning to every attorney who might refer a case to another attorney that you can't do so and avoid liability if Medicare compliance is ignored. The lesson is that when you refer a case to another firm you need to make sure you have three things: 1) a written fee agreement; 2) a copy of the lawyer's malpractice insurance policy declarations; and 3) proof that the lawyer has engaged a lien resolution firm or has a compliant process to resolve Medicare Conditional Payment obligations.

Similarly, in March of 2019, the United States Attorney for the District of Maryland announced that a Maryland personal injury law firm had agreed to pay the United States $250,000 to settle claims that it did not reimburse Medicare for payments made on behalf of the firm's client. As part of the settlement, the firm "also agreed to: (1) designate a person at the firm responsible for paying Medicare secondary payer debts; (2) train the designated employee to ensure that the firm pays these debts on a timely basis; and (3) review any outstanding debts with the designated employee at least every six months to ensure compliance."

Lastly, in June of 2018, the US Department of Justice announced a settlement with a Philadelphia Personal Injury Law Firm involving failure to reimburse Medicare. The firm agreed to start a "compliance program" and the DOJ stated that this "settlement agreement should remind personal injury lawyers and others of their obligation to reimburse Medicare for conditional payments after receiving settlement or judgment proceeds for their clients." The US Attorney's office also stated, "When an attorney fails to reimburse Medicare, the United States can recover from the attorney—even if the attorney already transmitted the proceeds to the client. Congress enacted these rules to ensure timely repayment from responsible parties, and we intend to hold attorneys accountable for failing to make good on their obligations."

Consequently, in today's complicated regulatory landscape, a comprehensive plan for Medicare compliance has become vitally important to personal injury practices. Lawyers assisting Medicare beneficiaries are personally exposed to damages and malpractice risks daily when they handle or resolve cases for

Medicare beneficiaries. The list of things to be concerned about is growing daily. The list includes things such as:

1. Not knowing what medical information/ICD codes are being reported by defendant insurers complying with Mandatory Insurer Reporting law[173] (MIR) created by MMSEA.[174]
2. Agreeing to onerous "Medicare Compliance" language that may be inapplicable or inaccurate, which binds the personal injury victim.
3. Failing to report and resolve conditional payment obligations leading to personal liability.
4. Not using processes to obtain money back from Medicare using the compromise and waiver process.
5. Failure to identify a lien, such as those asserted by Medicare Part C lienholders thereby exposing the personal injury lawyer and the firm to double damages.
6. Inadequate education of clients about Medicare compliance when it comes to "futures" and the risks of denial of future injury-related care.

So, what do you do? The answer is to develop a process to identify those who are Medicare beneficiaries in your practice and make sure that process is put into place to deal with the myriad of issues that can arise. The first step is education about these various issues to lawyers and their staff so problems can be identified before they become a malpractice issue or worse yet, a personal liability for any attorney involved in the matter. The following chapters focus on the educational component and offer sugges-

---

173 42 U.S.C. § 1395y(b)(7)-(8).

174 The MMSEA created a mandatory insurer reporting requirement which tasks defendants/ insurers with reporting settlements involving Medicare beneficiaries to Medicare. The reporting requirement requires settlements of $2,000 or greater to be reported as of 10/1/13. Medicare, Medicaid, and SCHIP Extension Act of 2007 (P.L. 110-173). This Act was passed by the House on December 19, 2007, and by a voice vote in the Senate on December 18, 2007.

tions for protecting your clients as well as your practice when it comes to dealing with clients who are part of the tort system and Medicare beneficiaries.

MEDICARE PROGRAM OVERVIEW

The Medicare program is made up of different parts.[175] Part A and Part B are thought of as traditional Medicare, which includes hospital insurance and medical insurance. Part A is the hospital insurance which covers inpatient care in hospitals and skilled nursing facilities (it does not cover custodial or long-term care—only Medicaid does). Part B benefits cover physician visits, durable medical equipment, and hospital outpatient care. It also covers some of the services Part A doesn't cover, such as physical and occupational therapies as well as some home healthcare. Part D is prescription drug coverage that is provided by private insurers approved by and funded by Medicare. Part C—Medicare Advantage Plans or MAOs, offers all of the coverages through Parts A, B, and D but through a private insurer approved by Medicare. It is an alternative to the service fees for Parts A and B coverages, which can be elected and purchased by a Medicare beneficiary.

There is a connection between Medicare eligibility and Social Security Disability Income (hereinafter SSDI). SSDI is the only way to get Medicare coverage prior to retirement age. This is pertinent as many injury victims become Medicare eligible by virtue of disability. Medicare and Social Security Disability Income benefits are an entitlement and are not income or asset sensitive like Medicaid/SSDI. Clients who meet Social Security's definition of

---

175 SSDI beneficiaries receive Part A Medicare benefits, which covers inpatient hospital services, home health, and hospice benefits. Part B benefits cover physicians' charges, and SSDI beneficiaries may obtain coverage by paying a monthly premium. Part D provides coverage for most prescription drugs, but it is a complicated system with a large copay called the donut hole.

disability and have paid in enough quarters into the system can receive disability benefits without regard to their financial situation.[176] The SSDI benefit program is funded by the workforce's contribution into FICA (Social Security) or self-employment taxes. Workers earn credits based on their work history and a worker must have enough credits to get SSDI benefits should they become disabled. Medicare is our federal health insurance program and as discussed above, is broken up into multiple parts. Medicare entitlement commences at age sixty-five or two years after becoming disabled under Social Security's definition of disability.

In conclusion, the government is very serious about and intent on enforcing the Medicare Secondary Payer Act. Failure by a lawyer to take appropriate actions with regard to reimbursement of Medicare when they make conditional payments, exposes that lawyer and his firm to potential enforcement actions by the government. Understanding the basics of the different parts to Medicare and its connection to SSDI is important as well. The following chapter addresses Mandatory Insurer Reporting and how that has provided the government with an incredible amount of information regarding all settlements of one thousand dollars or greater involving a current Medicare beneficiary.

---

176 While most often we deal with someone who has a disability, Social Security Disability also provides death benefits. Additionally, a child who became disabled before age twenty-two and has remained continuously disabled since age eighteen may receive disability benefits based on the work history of a disabled, deceased, or retired parent as long as the child is disabled and unmarried.

CHAPTER 7

THE MEDICARE SECONDARY PAYER ACT AND MANDATORY INSURER REPORTING

Representing someone who is Medicare eligible automatically triggers concerns over the implications of compliance with the Medicare Secondary Payer Act (hereinafter MSP). A client who is a current Medicare beneficiary or is reasonably expected to become one within thirty months should be educated about the MSP and protected from the ramifications of noncompliance. The MSP is a series of statutory provisions[177] enacted in 1980 as part of the Omnibus Reconciliation Act[178] with the goal of reducing federal healthcare costs. The MSP provides that if a primary payer exists, Medicare only pays for medical treatment relating to an injury to the extent that the primary payer does not pay.[179] The regulations that implement the MSP provide "[s]ection 1862(b)(2)(A)(ii) of the Act precludes Medicare payments for services to the extent that payment has been made or can reasonably be expected to be made promptly under any of the

---

177 The provisions of the MSP can be found at Section 1862(b) of the Social Security Act. 42 U.S.C. §
    1395y(b)(6) (2007).

178 Omnibus Reconciliation Act of 1980, Pub. L. No. 96-499 (Dec. 5, 1980).

179 42 CFR § 411.20(2) Part 411, Subpart B, (2007).

following": i) Workers' compensation; ii) Liability insurance; iii) No-fault insurance.[180]

There are two issues that arise when dealing with the application of the MSP: 1) Medicare payments made prior to the date of settlement (conditional payments); and 2) future Medicare payments for covered services (Medicare Set-Asides). According to CMS, both are obligations in terms of compliance with the MSP which extends to both prior to settlement and into the future. The passage of the Medicare, Medicaid, and SCHIP Extension Act of 2007 (MMSEA)[181] has triggered heightened concerns of all parties to a settlement involving a Medicare beneficiary. Part of this Act, Section 111,[182] extends the government's ability to enforce the Medicare Secondary Payer Act. As of April 1, 2011, a Responsible Reporting Entities/insurers (hereinafter RRE), (liability insurer, self-insurer, no-fault insurer, and workers' compensation carriers) must determine whether a claimant is a Medicare beneficiary ("entitled") and if so, provide certain information to the secretary of Health and Human Services (hereinafter "secretary") when the claim is resolved. This is the so-called Mandatory Insurer Requirement, MIR for short.[183]

Under MMSEA, the RRE must report the identity of the Medicare beneficiary to the secretary and other such information as the secretary deems appropriate to make a determination concerning coordination of benefits, including any applicable recovery of a claim. Failure of an applicable plan to comply with the reporting requirements potentially exposes them to a civil

---

180 *Id.*

181 Medicare, Medicaid, and SCHIP Extension Act of 2007 (P.L. 110-173).

182 42 U.S.C. § 1395y(b)(7)-(8).

183 *Id.*

money penalty for each day of noncompliance with respect to each claim.[184] These reporting requirements make it very easy for CMS to review settlements to determine whether Medicare's interests were adequately addressed by the settling parties and potentially deny future Medicare-covered services related to the injuries suffered.

The advent of MIR causes some very real and difficult problems for lawyers handling claims involving Medicare beneficiaries. For example, the biggest problem with the reporting requirement is the required disclosure of ICD medical diagnosis codes which identify the medical conditions that are injury related. These ICD codes can form the basis for the care potentially rejected by Medicare in the future. If the plaintiff and plaintiff's counsel are unaware of the conditions disclosed by the defendant/insurer through the reporting process, there could be some serious problems when the plaintiff seeks medical care from Medicare in the future. For example, a plaintiff sustained back and neck injuries which were claimed as a part of their lawsuit. The plaintiff had preexisting neck problems. The case is ultimately settled with the defendant paying nothing for the neck injury because they determined that the neck injury was primarily due to a preexisting condition. Now the defendant/insurer reports the settlement and lists the ICD-9 codes related to the neck injury even though they paid no settlement dollars toward that injury and rejected that part of the claim. The neck care could be rejected by Medicare in the future leaving the client with no Set-Aside funds to pay for that care and no Medicare coverage either. Worse yet, your ability to negotiate a conditional payment made by Medicare may be complicated by including care that is unrelated. This issue is further exacerbated by the reporting data being submitted by

---

184 *Id.*

outside reporting agents who are only providing initial case information without involvement of plaintiff's counsel.

Another example is when the date of accident that is reported doesn't match up with what the plaintiff reports. The MIR requirements don't relieve the personal injury lawyer's obligation to report through the BCRC and resolve the conditional payment. If the defendant insurer reports a date of accident that doesn't match with what was reported by plaintiff's counsel, it could trigger a second and new conditional payment demand from Medicare. This often leads to frustration and complication in resolving the conditional payment obligation.

Every time I am consulted by other lawyers about this issue, I suggest that the parties should be collaborating on this aspect of the Medicare settlement process. If the plaintiff does not know what is being reported, then the scenarios above could easily occur. The practical problem is that defense counsel typically is unaware of what is being reported and the ICD codes aren't included in the release. Accordingly, there are no guarantees that even if the parties discuss this aspect of the reporting conundrum that the right codes will be reported. However, it still bears emphasis and discussion. Without focusing on this issue as part of the settlement process, a plaintiff, plaintiff's lawyer, or an elder law attorney involved in the case may find there are serious unintended repercussions that result.

MMSEA/MIR RELEASE LANGUAGE

In this new age of hypervigilance surrounding Medicare compliance as a result of MIR, release language about protecting Medicare can be longer than the release itself. This language is frequently inaccurate or wholly inapplicable. In practice, I have seen language that mandates that the personal injury victim will not apply for Medicare or even Social Security Disability benefits. Equally as bad, language is frequently included that places a burden on the plaintiff to comply with requirements that aren't mandated by any law. Most of the language improperly cites statutes or regulations that don't say anything relevant to the issues at hand.

Therefore, great care needs to be taken by the personal injury practitioner in terms of what is agreed upon and included in the release. Technically, there is nothing required by any law that needs to be addressed in the release as it relates to the MSP. Practically speaking though, language has to be there to placate the other side's misinformation about their own liability regarding many of the MSP-related issues. It is simple to address these issues concisely and in a way that doesn't place any onerous obligations upon the plaintiff. Every case is different, and the facts dictate the use of a different language each time, but there is a core set of provisions that can be done in one simple paragraph to deal with the Medicare-related issues at hand.

MMSEA/MIR AND CONDITIONAL PAYMENTS

The stated intent of the new reporting requirements was to identify situations where Medicare should not be the primary payer and ultimately allow recovery of conditional payments. The Medicare Secondary Payer Act prohibits Medicare from making payments if payment has been made or is reasonably expected to be made by a workers' compensation plan, liability insurance, no fault insurance, or a group health plan.[185] However, Medicare may make a "conditional payment" if one of the

---

185   42 CFR § 411.20(2) Part 411, Subpart B, (2007).

aforementioned primary plans does not pay or can't be expected to be paid promptly.[186] These "conditional payments" are made subject to being repaid when the primary payer pays.[187] When conditional payments are made by Medicare, the government has a right of recovery against the settlement proceeds.[188]

The Medicare Secondary Payer Act and the Mandatory Insurer Reporting requirements form a complex set of issues that personal injury lawyers must deal with. As a result, realizing that every settlement with a Medicare beneficiary of one thousand dollars or more will be reported along with a variety of data points is critically important. Working collaboratively with the other side when it comes to these issues is recommended. Having incorrect or inaccurate information reported can cause issues for both your client and your law firm. The next chapter discusses how to effectively deal with resolving Medicare conditional payments.

---

186 42 U.S.C.S. § 1395y(b)(2)(B).

187 *Id.*

188 42 U.S.C.S. § 1395y(b)(2)(B)(iii).

CHAPTER 8

RESOLUTION OF MEDICARE CONDITIONAL PAYMENTS

Continuing with the exploration of Medicare Secondary Payer Act, we now turn our attention to Medicare Conditional Payments and resolution of those obligations. Congress has given the Centers for Medicare and Medicaid Services (hereinafter CMS) both subrogation rights and the right to bring an independent cause of action to recover its conditional payment from "any or all entities that are or were required or responsible...to make payment with respect to the same item or service (or any portion thereof) under a primary plan."[189] Furthermore, CMS is authorized under federal law to bring actions against "any other entity that has received payment from a primary plan."[190] Personal injury lawyers have been sued under this provision for failing to repay a Medicare lien. Most ominously, CMS may seek to recover double damages if it brings an independent cause of action.[191] Given all of the foregoing, Medicare subrogation law is a problematic area for personal injury practitioners. The

---

189 42 U.S.C. § 1395y(b)(2)(B)(iii) (2007).

190 *Id.*

191 42 U.S.C. § 1395y(b)(2)(B)(iii) (2007).

MSPA[192] presents liability concerns for personal injury practitioners because of its complexity, and the difficulty in dealing with Medicare's subrogation bureaucracy.[193]

As discussed in chapter 6, the government is very serious about its reimbursement rights when it comes to Medicare conditional payments. As an example, in *U.S. v. Harris*, a November 2008 opinion, a personal injury plaintiff lawyer lost his motion to dismiss against the US Government in a suit involving the failure to satisfy a Medicare subrogation claim.[194] The plaintiff, the United States of America, filed for declaratory judgment and money damages against the personal injury attorney owed to the Centers for Medicare and Medicaid Services by virtue of third-party payments made to a Medicare beneficiary.[195] The personal injury attorney had settled a claim for a Medicare beneficiary (James Ritchea) for $25,000.[196] Medicare had made conditional payments in the amount of $22,549.67. After settlement, plaintiff's counsel sent Medicare the details of the settlement and Medicare calculated they were owed approximately $10,253.59 out of the $25,000.[197] Plaintiff's counsel failed to pay this amount and the government filed suit.

A motion to dismiss filed by plaintiff's counsel was denied by the United States District Court for the Northern District of West

---

192 42 U.S.C. § 1395y(b)(2)(B).

193 For a good discussion of the issues relating to conditional payments, *see* Jonathan Allan Klein & Annmarie M. Liermann, *Medicare Lien Interests in Liability Settlements—Easy Solutions to Help Resolve Medicare Reimbursement Issues for Beneficiaries and Insurers*, Medicare Secondary Payer Act Reform Task Force (2007).

194 *U.S. v. Harris*, No. 5:08CV102, 2009 WL 891931 (N.D. W.Va. Mar. 26, 2009), *aff'd* 334 Fed. Appx 569 (4th Cir. 2009).

195 *Id.* at *1.

196 *Id.*

197 *Id.*

Virginia despite plaintiff counsel's arguments that he had no personal liability. Plaintiff's counsel argued that he could not be held liable individually under 42 U.S.C. 1395y(b)(2) because he forwarded the details of the settlement to the government and thus the settlement funds were distributed to his clients with the government's knowledge and consent. The court disagreed. The court pointed out that the government may under 42 U.S.C. 1395y(b)(2)(B)(iii) "recover under this clause from any entity that has received payment from a primary plan or from the proceeds of a primary plan's payment to any entity." Further, the court pointed to the federal regulations implementing the MSPS which state that CMS has a right of action to recover its payments from any entity including an attorney.[198] Subsequently, the US Government filed a motion for summary judgment against plaintiff's counsel. The United States District Court, in March of 2009, granted the motion for summary judgment against plaintiff's counsel and held that the government was entitled to a judgment in the amount of $11,367.78 plus interest.[199]

Resolution of the government's interests concerning conditional payment obligations is simple in application but time consuming. The process of reporting the settlement starts with contacting the Benefits Coordination Recovery Contractor (BCRC).[200] This starts prior to settlement so that you can obtain and review a conditional payment letter (CPL).[201] These letters are preliminary and can't be relied upon to pay Medicare from. However, they are necessary to review and audit for removal of unrelated

---

198 *See* 42 C.F.R. 411.24 (g).

199 *U.S. v. Harris,* No. 5:08CV102, 2009 WL 891931 at *5.

200 *See* https://www.cms.gov/Medicare/Coordination-of-Benefits-and-Recovery/Attorney-Services/Attorney-Services.html.

201 *See* https://www.cms.gov/Medicare/Coordination-of-Benefits-and-Recovery/Attorney-Services/Conditional-Payment-Information/Conditional-Payment-Information.html.

care. Once settlement is achieved, Medicare must be given the details regarding settlement so they can issue a final demand. Once the final demand is issued, Medicare must be paid its final demand amount regardless of whether an appeal, compromise, or waiver is sought.[202] Paying the final demand amount within sixty days of issuance is required or interest begins to accrue at over 10 percent and ultimately it is referred to the US Treasury for an enforcement action to recover the unpaid amount if not addressed.[203]

RESOLUTION OF CONDITIONAL PAYMENTS—APPEAL, COMPROMISE, OR WAIVER

The repayment formula for Medicare is set by the Code of Federal Regulations. 411.37(c) & (d) prescribes a reduction for procurement costs.[204] The formula doesn't take into account liability-related issues in the case, caps on damages, or policy limits. The end result can be that the entire settlement must be used to reimburse Medicare. The only alternative is to appeal, which requires you to go through four levels of internal Medicare appeals before you ever have the opportunity to appear before a federal judge to argue for a compromise/waiver. There is plenty of case law requiring exhaustion of the internal Medicare appeals processes, which means that Medicare appeals are a lengthy and unattractive resolution method.[205] What makes them even more

---

202 *Id.*

203 42 C.F.R. 411.24(m).

204 42 C.F.R. 411.37(c) & (d).

205 A perfect example of this is *Alcorn v. Pepples* out of the Western District of Kentucky. In *Alcorn*, the court held that "Alcorn's claim with respect to the Secretary arises under the Medicare Act because it rests on the repayment obligations set forth under 42 U.S.C. § 1395y. She therefore must exhaust the administrative remedies established under the Medicare Act before this court may exercise subject matter jurisdiction over her claim." *Alcorn v. Pepples*, 2011 U.S. Dist. LEXIS 19627 (W.D. Ky. Feb. 25, 2011).

unattractive is the fact that interest continues to accrue during the appeal as long as the final demand amount remains unpaid.

An alternative resolution method is to request a compromise or waiver post-payment of the final demand. By paying Medicare their final demand and requesting a compromise/ waiver, the interest meter stops running. If Medicare grants a compromise or waiver, they actually issue a refund back to the Medicare beneficiary. There are three viable ways to request a compromise/ waiver. The first is via Section 1870(c) of the Social Security Act, which is the financial hardship waiver and is evaluated by the BCRC.[206] The second is via section 1862(b) of the Social Security Act, which is the "best interest of the program" waiver and is evaluated by CMS itself.[207] The third way is under the Federal Claims Collection Act and the compromise request is evaluated by CMS.[208] If any of these are successfully granted, Medicare will refund the amount that was paid via the final demand or a portion thereof depending on whether it is a full waiver or just a compromise.

To summarize, resolution of a Medicare conditional payment is achieved either by following the reduction formulas found in the Code of Federal Regulations or by appeal, waiver, and/or compromise. There are multiple considerations before deciding to appeal or seek a compromise/waiver of conditional payments. Certain steps are necessary to resolve a conditional payment, which includes audit/verification of the amount after receiving the conditional payment letter and securing a final demand by providing final settlement details to Medicare. Failure to resolve

206 42 U.S.C. § 1395gg.

207 42 U.S.C § 1395y.

208 31 U.S.C. § 3711.

a conditional payment exposes a trial lawyer to personal liability for the amount of the conditional payment and the government does pursue lawyers individually if they fail to reimburse Medicare. The following chapter details the concerns raised when a client has opted into a Part C Medicare Advantage Plan and they then have a lien against the settlement.

CHAPTER 9

RESOLUTION OF PART C MEDICARE ADVANTAGE (MAO) LIENS

In the previous chapter, Medicare conditional payment resolution was explored. Some clients, post-accident, may have switched over to a Part C Medicare Advantage Plan. Therefore, even if you have gone through the resolution process for your client and gotten the Medicare conditional payment-related issues dealt with you might not be finished. What lurks out there is that a Part C Advantage Plan (hereinafter MAO) may have paid for some or all of your client's care. You may wonder how that is possible when you were told that the client was a Medicare beneficiary and Part A/B was paid back for conditional payments. The reason is that MAOs aren't Medicare, and injury victim clients can elect to enroll in an MAO during relevant enrollment periods. Therefore, a MAO may have made payments after election of which you are completely unaware. Neither Medicare, BCRC, nor CMS will alert you to this fact, nor do they have any information as it relates to MAOs. Therefore, attorneys handling matters that involve a Medicare beneficiary must be vigilant and do their own due diligence to track down possible MAO liens or face the possibility of having to personally pay the lien times two. Although shocking, it is an area of the law that is rapidly developing in favor of MAO plans.

MAO plans use the Medicare Secondary Payer statute as the basis for their claims to reimbursement.[209] Accordingly, their repayment formulas are the same as Medicare under 411.37 (c) and (d), which only requires a procurement cost reduction. That being said, these plans are typically willing to negotiate and arguably must provide a mechanism for a compromise or waiver if they avail themselves of the MSP in terms of their recovery rights. All of that is well and good, but what happens when you don't know that an MAO has a lien? The answer is fairly ominous for all the parties to a personal injury settlement. A private cause of action can be brought as an enforcement action for double the amount of the lien. This right is provided for in the Medicare Secondary Payer Act itself. While parties have long been afraid of the government using this provision, it is on behalf of the MAOs that these actions are now being brought effectively to enforce their reimbursement rights times two.

According to the MSP, a private cause of action exists when a primary plan fails to reimburse a secondary plan for the conditional payments it has made. "There is established a private cause of action for damages (which shall be in an amount double the amount otherwise provided) in the case of a primary plan which fails to provide for primary payment (or appropriate reimbursement) in accordance with paragraphs (1) and (2)(A)."[210] 42 C.F.R. §422.108(f) extends the private cause of action to Medicare Advantage Plans. "MAOs will exercise the same rights to recover from a primary plan, entity, or individual that the Secretary exercises under the MSP regulations in subparts B through D of part 411 of this chapter." According to 42 C.F.R. §411.24(g), "CMS has

---

209 An MAO "will exercise the same rights to recover from a primary plan, entity, or individual that the Secretary exercises under the MSP regulations in subparts B through D of part 411 of this chapter." 42 C.F.R. § 422.108(f).

210 42 U.S.C. § 1395y(b)(3)(A).

a right of action to recover its payments from any entity, including a beneficiary, provider, supplier, physician, attorney, state agency or private insurer that has received a primary payment." Case in point: a plaintiff personal injury law firm was sued last year by Humana for a $191,000 lien that wasn't repaid because the firm was unaware of the lien. The damages claimed were $382,000 which is precisely double the lien that wasn't paid. That case was resolved confidentially out of court.

The seminal case on this issue is, for now, *Humana v. Western Heritage Ins. Co.*,[211] from late 2016. This was a slip-and-fall case wherein just before settlement the existence of a Humana Medicare Advantage plan was discovered.[212] Western Heritage, the defendant insurer, initially put Humana on the settlement check but a state court judge ordered it removed.[213] The plaintiff failed to repay Humana, so Humana initiated litigation directly against the defendant insurer.[214] Western Heritage placed the amount of Humana's demand in trust during the litigation and disclosed the existence and location to Humana.[215] The Eleventh Circuit Court of Appeals granted Humana's Motion for Summary Judgment and held that Humana's right to reimbursement for the conditional payments it made on behalf of the plan beneficiary under a Medicare Advantage Plan was enforceable.[216] Western Heritage had an obligation to independently reimburse Humana. When they failed to do so, the court ruled that as a matter of law, Humana was entitled to maintain a private cause of action

---

211 *Humana Medical Plan, Inc. v. Western Heritage Insurance Company*, 832 F. 3d 1229 (11th Cir. 2016).

212 *Id.* at 1232.

213 *Id.*

214 *Id.*

215 *Id.*

216 *Id.* at 1239.

for double damages pursuant to 42 U.S.C. § 1395y(b)(3)(A) and was therefore entitled to $38,310.82 in damages.[217] The Eleventh Circuit said that placing the $19,155.41 in trust was not the same as paying the MAO and that the damages "SHALL" be double.[218]

In summary, when it comes to MAO liens there is a good chance you may be unaware that a lien exists without your own research. A good practice is to obtain copies of all government assistance program cards and any health insurance cards to see just what the injury victim is receiving in terms of benefits/insurance coverage. Make sure a thorough investigation is done if the client is a Medicare beneficiary for the existence of Part C/MAO liens. The investigation and inquiry should start upon intake and continue throughout representation with the final check occurring before disbursement of settlement proceeds. Failing to do so may expose you and your firm to personal liability for double damages to a Part C Plan or Medicare itself. Once a Part C/MAO lien is identified, you must aggressively pursue reduction methods either using traditional lien reduction arguments if the MAO doesn't insist upon adherence to the MSP or using the MSP's compromise or waiver provisions.

---

217 *Id.* at 1240.

218 *Id.*

CHAPTER 10

MEDICARE FUTURES

THE UNREGULATED NEW FRONTIER

Chapters 6 through 9 focused primarily on the issues with conditional payments/liens and Mandatory Insurer Reporting. While those issues are very important, a larger issue looms regarding payments made by Medicare after settlement. Today, there is a very real threat of Medicare denying future injury-related care after the personal injury case is resolved. This can be very easily triggered by the MIR and reporting of injury-related ICD codes, which happens automatically now with any settlement of one thousand dollars or greater. Once a denial of care is triggered, a Medicare beneficiary has to go through the four levels of internal Medicare appeals plus a federal district court before ever getting the denial of care addressed by a federal appeals court. This is why it must be of primary concern for the personal injury practitioner to address these issues, particularly in catastrophic injury cases where denial of care could be devastating to the injury victim's medical quality of life.

In the past, trial lawyers never had to worry about whether Medicare would pay for their client's future care post-settlement. There is cause for concern that this may not be the case in the future. Consider this scenario: You represent a current Medicare beneficiary in a third-party liability case. As part of the workup of the case, you determine the client will need future medical care related to the injuries suffered. This could be determined by either deposing the treating physician, or by the creation of a life-care plan for litigation purposes. Ultimately, you settle the case. Since the client is a Medicare beneficiary, the defendant will report the settlement under the Mandatory Insurer Reporting law as it is greater than $750 in gross settlement proceeds. The defendant puts some language into the release about a Medicare Set-Aside being the injury victim's responsibility and that they can't shift the burden. Everyone signs the release and settlement dollars are paid. The file is closed, then forgotten. What happens though if that course of action triggers a denial of future care by Medicare?

For many years this was not even a concern for trial attorneys and their clients. However, the risk of this occurring is now a very real possibility. In fact, in 2018, a personal injury victim got this type of notice of denial for injury-related care from Medicare. The service provided was hospital outpatient clinic services under Part B of Medicare. The bill was denied, based upon the notice, because Medicare said, "you may have funds set aside from your settlement to pay for your future medical expenses and prescription drug treatment related to your injury(ies)." The denial was related to a 2014 personal injury settlement wherein the Medicare beneficiary was paid money as damages for future injury-related care. Medicare's position that an injury victim can't settle their case and shift the burden to the Medicare Trust Fund for injury-related care isn't new. Medicare has stated this premise over and over. This was the first time anyone had seen an actual denial.

Unfortunately, there is no cookie-cutter answer for what to do about Medicare compliance. It is a case-by-case analysis. In some instances, there may be an argument that future medicals aren't funded at all by the settlement. In other cases, there might be an argument that a reduced amount of future medicals should be set aside to satisfy obligations under the MSP because the case settled for less than full value. There are just too many possibilities to give a simple, one-size-fits-all answer. However, what is clear is that doing nothing has its risks. For example, the client who received the denial of care likely will face a lengthy appeal process within Medicare that must be exhausted before having the issue addressed by a federal district court. In that scenario, the client is going to have to decide between paying out of their own pocket for future care or waiting for the care until exhausting all appeals in anticipation of prevailing over Medicare.

While the problem created for the client is a serious one if they are denied care, an equally scary proposition for the trial lawyer is their exposure for malpractice claims in this scenario. Let's assume that the injury victim who got this denial letter was not properly advised of the risks of failing to set aside money. Would the trial lawyer potentially face a suit for legal malpractice? The answer is most likely they would. There could be all sorts of arguments made about whether they fell below the standard of care, but in the end, this is a known issue and one that is of the law. Worse yet, a trial lawyer and his/her firm could have Medicare breathing down their necks. While we haven't see any instances of Medicare pursuing a law firm over failing to set up a Medicare Set-Aside, as discussed earlier, there are recent examples of law firms being pursued by the Department Of Justice (DOJ) related to other aspects of the MSP and failing to have a process internally to insure compliance with the MSP.

When it comes to Set-Asides, there are a few key takeaways from this portion of the book. First, you only have to worry about this issue if you are dealing with someone who is a current Medicare beneficiary or arguably those with a reasonable expectation of becoming one within thirty months. The latter includes those who have applied for or begun receiving Social Security Disability benefits. At time of publishing, there is no regulation, statute, or case law requiring a Medicare Set-Aside to deal with futures. Instead, it has become analogous to the situation in resolving cases with those who are on Medicaid or SSI. In those cases, a client must be educated about the opportunity to set up a Special Needs Trust to remain eligible for needs-based benefits. Similarly, a Medicare beneficiary should be informed about the opportunity to set up a Medicare Set-Aside to protect future Medicare eligibility for injury-related care. The good news for attorneys assisting Medicare beneficiaries, is that a Medicare Set-Aside allocation can be used in an offensive manner to set the floor for medical damages in a case.

All of that being said, you might be wondering why even consider doing a Medicare Set-Aside when they aren't required by any law? The answer is that actually setting anything aside is less important than doing the legal analysis to determine why anything should be set aside. Said a different way, this is a plaintiff issue and not a defense issue. The only penalty for failing to address this issue is the potential loss of future Medicare coverage for injury-related care. You ultimately want to educate the client on the risks of failing to do a Set-Aside analysis and then document that education in your file. The next question might be: What risk is there if there isn't any law requiring Set-Asides? Again, the answer boils down to CMS' interpretation of the MSP. According to CMS, since Medicare isn't supposed to pay for future medical expenses covered by a liability or workers' compensation settlement, judgment, or award, it *recommends* that injury victims set aside a sufficient amount of a personal injury settlement to cover future medical expenses that are Medicare covered. CMS' "recommended" way to protect future Medicare benefit eligibility is establishment of an MSA to pay for injury-related care until exhaustion.[219]

WHY AND HOW DID CMS COME UP WITH MSAS?

For many years, personal injury cases have been resolved without consideration of Medicare's secondary payer status even though since 1980 all forms of liability insurance have been primary to Medicare. At settlement, by judgment or through an award, an injury victim would receive damages for future medical expenses that were Medicare covered. However, none of those settlement dollars would be used to pay for future Medicare-covered health needs. Instead, the burden would be shifted from the primary payer (liability insurer or workers' compensation carrier) to Medicare. Injury victims would routinely provide their Medicare card to providers for injury-related care.

These practices began to change in 2001 when Set-Asides were officially developed by CMS as a MSP compliance tool for workers' compensation cases. Interestingly, around that same time the General Accounting Office was studying the Medicare system and pointed out that Medicare was losing money by paying for care that was covered under the workers' compensation system.[220] Accordingly, CMS circulated a memo in 2001 to all its

---

219 Sally Stalcup, MSP Regional Coordinator (May 2011 Handout). *See also*, Charlotte Benson, *Medicare Secondary Payer—Liability Insurance (Including Self-Insurance) Settlements, Judgments, Awards, or Other Payments and Future Medicals—INFORMATION*, Centers for Medicare and Medicaid Services Memorandum, September 29, 2011.

220 Edward M. Welch, *Medicare and Worker's Compensation After the 2003 Amendments,* Workers' Compensation Policy Review, at 5 (March/April 2003).

regional offices announcing that compliance with the Medicare Secondary Payer Act required claimants to set aside a portion of their settlement for future Medicare-covered expenses where the settlement closed out future medical expenses.[221] The new "Set-Aside" requirement was designed to prevent attempts "to shift liability for the cost of a work-related injury or illness to Medicare."[222] Set-Asides ensure that Medicare does not pay for future medical care that is being compensated by a primary payer by way of a settlement or an award.

To summarize, a Medicare beneficiary who settles their case and attempts to shift the burden to Medicare to pay for future injury-related care might be denied coverage by Medicare. Medicare interprets the Medicare Secondary Payer Act as requiring consideration of their "future interests." While Set-Asides are not required by a statute or regulation, they are a creature of CMS policy. Failing to address this issue can result in a future denial of injury-related care by Medicare. The following chapter goes into greater detail about what a Medicare Set-Aside is and how they work, as well as a discussion about the "regulatory" scheme.

---

221 Parashar B. Patel, *Medicare Secondary Payer Statute: Medicare Set-Aside Arrangements*, Centers for Medicare and Medicaid Services Memorandum, July 23, 2001.

222 *Id.*

CHAPTER 11

MEDICARE FUTURES

WHAT IS A MEDICARE SET-ASIDE?

Before getting into an overview of the regulatory environment of MSAs, it is first important to explain exactly what a Set-Aside is. An MSA is a portion of settlement proceeds set aside, called an "allocation," to pay for future Medicare-covered services that must be exhausted prior to Medicare paying for any future care related to the injury.[223] The amount of the Set-Aside is determined on a case-by-case basis and is submitted to CMS for approval if it is a workers' compensation case and fits within the review thresholds established by CMS. CMS' review and approval process is voluntary.[224] There are no formal guidelines for submission of liability settlements and the CMS regional offices determine whether or not to review liability submissions (presently, most do not review). CMS explains on its website that the purpose of a Medicare Set-Aside is to "pay for all services related to the claimant's work-related injury or disease, therefore, Medicare will not make any payments (as a primary, secondary, or tertiary payer) for any services related to the work-related injury or disease until nothing

---

223 *See* https://www.cms.gov/Medicare/Coordination-of-Benefits-and-Recovery/Workers-Compensation-Medicare-Set-Aside-Arrangements/WCMSA-Overview.html.

224 *Id.*

remains in the WCMSA."[225] According to CMS, the Set-Aside is meant to pay for all work-injury-related medical expenses, not just portions of those future medical expenses.

REGULATORY "SCHEME"—WHAT, IF ANY, "LAW" IS THERE FOR SET-ASIDES IN PERSONAL INJURY SETTLEMENTS?

A formal Medicare Set-Aside is not required by a federal statute even in workers' compensation cases where they have been commonplace since 2001. Instead, CMS has intricate guidelines and FAQs on their website for nearly every aspect of Set-Asides from when to do one, to submission, to administration for workers' compensation settlements.[226] There are limited guidelines for liability settlements involving Medicare beneficiaries. Without codification of Set-Asides, there are no clear-cut appellate procedures from arbitrary CMS decisions and no definitive rules one can count on as it relates to Medicare Set-Asides. While there is no legal requirement that an MSA be created, the failure to do so may result in Medicare refusing to pay for future medical expenses related to the injury until the entire settlement is exhausted. There has been a slow progression toward a CMS policy of creating Set-Asides in liability settlements as a result of the MMSEA's passage and the onset of MIR. This culminated with the presumed codification of formal regulations back in 2014.[227] However, without explanation, those regulations were withdrawn after having gone through significant vetting along with public commentary. The apparent reason was complaints from both sides about the fairness and workability in practice of the proposed regulations.

---

225 *Id.*

226 *See* https://www.cms.gov/Medicare/Coordination-of-Benefits-and-Recovery/Workers-Compensation-Medicare-Set-Aside-Arrangements/WCMSA-Memorandums/Memorandums.html.

227 77 F.R. 35917; http://www.gpo.gov/fdsys/pkg/FR-2012-06-15/pdf/2012-14678.pdf.

In 2016, it became evident that CMS was not fazed by previous failed attempts at codification of rules for Set-Asides in liability cases and was determined to develop a process to avoid shifting the burden to Medicare post-resolution of a personal injury settlement. The Department of Health and Human Services issued its budget for 2017 that included a line item indicating CMS had requested legislative authority to pursue a new policy regarding the treatment of future medicals.[228] In June of 2016, CMS issued an alert that they were considering expanding their voluntary review process to liability cases.[229] Thereafter, CMS sought proposals for a new review contractor for Set-Asides that included the anticipated review of 51,000 liability proposed Set-Asides annually.[230] In 2017, Medicare sent a memorandum to its contractors indicating that Medicare and its contractors will reject medical claims submitted post-resolution of a liability settlement on the basis that those claims "should be paid from a Liability Medicare Set-Aside (LMSA)."[231]

---

228 Medicare beneficiaries are unable to satisfy Medicare Secondary Payer "Future Medical" obligations at the time of settlement, judgment, award, or other payment because the current law does not specifically permit the secretary to deposit such payment in the Medicare Trust Funds. Future Medical is defined as Medicare-covered and otherwise reimbursable items and/or services furnished after the date of settlement, judgment, award, or other payment. This proposal expands current Medicare Secondary Payer statutory authority to permit the secretary to deposit into the Medicare Trust Funds a lump sum, upfront payment from beneficiaries when they obtain liability insurance, no-fault insurance, and workers' compensation settlements, judgments, awards, or other payments. [$65 million in savings over ten years] https://www.hhs.gov/about/budget/fy2017/budget-in-brief/cms/medicare/index.html.

229 "June 8, 2016—Consideration for Expansion of Medicare Set-Aside Arrangements (MSA). The Centers for Medicare and Medicaid Services (CMS) is considering expanding its voluntary Medicare Set-Aside Arrangements (MSA) amount review process to include the review of proposed liability insurance (including self-insurance) and no-fault insurance MSA amounts. CMS plans to work closely with the stakeholder community to identify how best to implement this potential expansion. CMS will provide future announcements of the proposal and expects to schedule town hall meetings later this year. Please continue to monitor this website for additional updates." https://www.cms.gov/Medicare/Coordination-of-Benefits-and-Recovery/Coordination-of-Benefits-and-Recovery-Overview/Whats-New/Whats-New.html.

230 https://www.fbo.gov/index?s=opportunity&mode=form&id=f1ae2d5eb785ac35d331eecc4d001ebb&tab=core&tabmode=list&=.

231 https://www.cms.gov/Outreach-and-Education/Medicare-Learning-Network-MLN/MLNMattersArticles/downloads/MM9893.pdf.

Late in the fall of 2018, the Office of Management and Budget issued a notification from the Department of Health and Human Services, which oversees CMS of a proposed rule related to the MSP. The abstract of the rule says it "would ensure that beneficiaries are making the best healthcare choices possible by providing them and their representatives with the opportunity to select an option for meeting future medical obligations that fits their individual circumstances, while also protecting the Medicare Trust Fund."[232] It indicated that the rule was "economically significant" and the basis for the legal authority was 42 U.S.C. 1396y(b). The final rule was expected sometime in 2019 but hasn't yet materialized.

All the foregoing considered, while there is no regulation or statute requiring anything be done when it comes to Set-Asides, ignoring the issue isn't the answer. It is obvious that Medicare interprets the MSP as preventing shifting the burden from a primary payer to Medicare post-resolution of a personal injury settlement. The problem is: how do you do that in a liability settlement given the issues that cause those cases to frequently settle for less than full value? There is no good answer to that question. However, there are cases that have addressed a couple of very important issues in that regard. While they are only trial court orders, they are instructive in terms of how to deal with the issues. The following chapter explores some of the trial court orders that exist and discusses their importance.

---

[232] https://www.reginfo.gov/public/do/eAgendaViewRule?pubId=201810&RIN=0938-AT85.

CHAPTER 12

MEDICARE FUTURES

NOTEWORTHY CASES

As discussed in the previous chapter, there are no real hard and fast rules when it comes to Set-Asides since they are not codified in the law. This has resulted in parties addressing these issues by court orders when settling cases involving Medicare beneficiaries. The first case of note is the most dangerous since it is frequently misinterpreted. Many lawyers have said that the *Aranki v. Burwell* decision holds that MSAs are not required in liability settlements and that these issues need not be addressed at all.[233] The former is accurate, but the latter assertion could not be further from the truth. In *Aranki*, the parties sought to have a federal district court declare there was no obligation to set anything aside. The court said "[n]o federal law or CMS regulation requires the creation of a MSA in personal injury settlements to cover potential future medical expenses."[234] The court did not determine that Medicare's future interest could be ignored. The court echoed existing CMS memoranda in finding that an MSA is not required by any statute or regulation. Most importantly, nothing in the opinion precludes

---

233 *Aranki v. Burwell*, 151 F.Supp.3d 1038 (D. Az. 2015).

234 *Id.*

Medicare from denying future injury-related care based upon information reported to CMS as part of MIR. The nuance of this case should be considered carefully, because it certainly does not represent a "get-out-of-jail-free card" in regard to these issues and Medicare can always deny care.

One of the big issues that can arise in trying to do a Set-Aside is the question of funding of future medicals. Funding of future medicals is a prerequisite to any type of Set-Aside analysis in the first place. The first question always asked is whether the client is a current Medicare beneficiary or has a reasonable expectation of becoming one within thirty months. If the answer is no, there is no need for a Set-Aside analysis. Similarly, if future medicals aren't funded then there is no need to engage in a Set-Aside analysis.

The issue of funding of future medicals was addressed by a Connecticut state court. In *Sterrett v. Klebart* (Conn. Super. Ct. Feb. 4, 2013), the court was asked to decide whether Medicare's interests were reasonably considered pursuant to the Medicare Secondary Payer Act.[235] The Connecticut court found that future medicals were not funded in this case due to competing claims. Specifically, the court stated that "the settlement payment to Sterrett does not address any future medical expenses that may be covered by Medicare and the facts of this case mandate the conclusion that the defendants and their carriers lack liability with regard to any such expenses."[236] The court found that the settlement represented a "substantial compromise" considering the potential verdict range.[237] The settlement was a compromise

---

235 *Sterrett v. Klebart*, 2013 Conn. Super. LEXIS 245 (Conn. Super. Ct. Feb. 4, 2013).

236 *Id.*

237 *Id.*

due to the nature of the injuries and defenses according to the court. Further, the court understood that even though Sterrett would incur medical bills payable by Medicare, the settlement didn't compensate for such future medical benefits.[238] Instead, the limited settlement funds it found were payable for the plaintiff's noneconomic damages with a small portion to be used for non-Medicare-covered economic damages.[239] For those reasons, the court held that no Set-Aside was required and found that the parties had reasonably considered the interests of Medicare in the settlement of the case.[240]

The really problematic issue is how do you deal with cases where future medicals are funded but they were settled for pennies on the dollar? Can you apportion the settlement so that you create a reduction formula tied to a comparison of the full value of damages versus what was actually recovered? For example, if the total value of the damages was $1 million but only $100,000 was recovered due to policy limits, can you set aside only 10 percent instead of 100 percent of the value of future medical expenses that are Medicare-covered related to the injuries suffered? This issue was addressed by a federal district court in 2013. In *Benoit v. Neustrom* (W.D. La. 2013), the United States District Court for the Western District of Louisiana rendered an unprecedented decision.[241] In a case where a limited recovery was achieved due to complicated liability issues with the case, the court reduced a liability Medicare Set-Aside allocation by applying a reduction methodology.

---

238 *Id.*

239 *Id.*

240 *Id.*

241 *Benoit v. Neustrom*, 2013 U.S. Dist. LEXIS 55971 (W.D. La. 2013).

The *Benoit* case was settled in October of 2012, conditioned upon a full release by Mr. Benoit and his assumption of sole responsibility for "protecting and satisfying the interests of Medicare and Medicaid." To that end, a Medicare Set-Aside allocation was prepared by an MSA vendor. The MSA cost projections gave a range of future Medicare-covered, injury-related care of $277,758 to $333,267. The gross settlement amount was $100,000. Medicaid agreed to waive its lien. Medicare asserted a reimbursement right for its conditional payments of $2,777.88. After payment of fees, costs, and the Medicare conditional payment, Mr. Benoit was left with net proceeds of $55,707.98. Mr. Benoit filed a motion for Declaratory Judgment confirming the terms of the settlement agreement, calculating the future potential medical expenses for treatment of his injuries in compliance with the Medicare Secondary Payer Act and representing to the court that the settlement amount was insufficient to provide a Set-Aside totaling 100 percent of the MSA.

The matter was set for hearing and Medicare was put on notice of the hearing. Medicare responded with a written letter asserting its demand for repayment of the conditional payment in the amount of $2,777.88 but didn't address the Set-Aside. Having heard testimony, the court rendered its opinion in April of 2013. The court made its findings of fact and conclusions of law, which were not worthy of mention aside from the bombshell finding that the net settlement was 18.2 percent of the midpoint range of the MSA projection and using that percentage as applied to the net settlement, the sum to be set aside was $10,138 and not $305,512. The court found that $10,138 adequately protected Medicare's interests.[242]

---

242 *Id.*

In its conclusions of law, the court first found it had jurisdiction to decide the motion because there was "an actual controversy and the parties seek a declaration as to their rights and obligations in order to comply with the MSP and its attendant regulations in the context of a third party settlement for which there is no procedure in place by CMS."[243] The court then found that the sum of $10,138 "reasonably and fairly takes Medicare's interests into account."[244] Lastly, the court found that since CMS provides no procedure to determine the adequacy of protecting Medicare's interests for future medical needs in third-party claims and since there is a strong public policy interest in resolving lawsuits through settlement, Medicare's interests were "adequately protected in this settlement within the meaning of the MSP."[245] The court ordered that the MSA be funded out of the settlement proceeds and be deposited into an interest-bearing account to be self-administered by Mr. Benoit's wife.

This opinion is so important because it hits the nail on the head regarding an argument I have been making since the advent of liability MSAs. As both sides have pointed out to CMS in vetting proposed regulations for liability Set-Asides, a liability insurer is not legally obligated to provide medical care in the future whereas workers' compensation carriers are obligated to pay for future medical if the injury-related conditions persist. Furthermore, liability settlements are fundamentally different from workers' compensation settlements in that liability cases are settled for a variety of reasons, which do not necessarily include contemplation of future medical treatment. Even when future medical care is contemplated as part of a settlement, the amount

---

243 *Id.*

244 *Id.*

245 *Id.*

can be very limited when compared to what the ultimate costs may end up being. So accordingly, if Set-Asides are done in liability settlements without recognition of these differences and with no apportionment of damages, you can conceivably have a situation where a party is setting aside their entire net settlement even though it is made up of nonmedical damages. In effect, it can eliminate the recovery of the nonmedical portion of the damages by requiring the Medicare beneficiary to set aside all of their net proceeds. There is nothing in the MSP regulations or statute that requires Medicare to seek 100 percent reimbursement of future medicals when the injury victim recovers substantially less than his or her full measure of damages.

A REDUCTION METHOD BASED ON BENOIT AND AHLBORN IDEOLOGY

As discussed above in the *Benoit* case, there has to be a framework to address settlements that do not make a plaintiff whole in the context of liability MSAs. Obliviously, it does not work to have 100 percent of a settlement consumed by a Medicare Set-Aside that the client can't touch except to pay for future Medicare-covered services. I would argue that this gets to the very root of the issue dealt with in the US Supreme Court decision in *Arkansas Department of Health and Human Services v. Ahlborn*.[246] The *Ahlborn* decision forbids lien recovery by Medicaid state agencies against the nonmedical portion of the settlement or judgment. While admittedly that decision dealt with Medicaid lien issues and the Medicaid anti-lien statute, the arguments by analogy can be applied in the Medicare Set-Aside context. The *Ahlborn* holding gets at the fundamental issue of whether a lien can be asserted against the nonmedical portion of a personal injury recovery. Justice Stevens, in stating the majority opinion, said

---

246 Ahlborn, 547 U.S. 268 (2006); see *The ElderLaw Report*, June 2006, p. 6.

"a rule of absolute priority might preclude settlement in a large number of cases, and be unfair to the recipient in others." Isn't this so in the Medicare Set-Aside context (which is really a future lien)? How do you settle a case for an injury victim when all of the proceeds would have to go into a Set-Aside? Wouldn't that force cases to trial where damages could be allocated to different aspects of the claim and a larger recovery might be possible?

In addition, the Eleventh Circuit *Bradley* decision addressed the issue of Medicare's lien rights in the context of Florida's wrongful death statute.[247] In *Bradley*, CMS took the position that only an allocation on the merits of a case would be recognized in terms of reducing a Medicare conditional payment obligation. The Eleventh Circuit approved a probate court's equitable distribution findings to reduce the Medicare conditional payment obligation. In so doing, the court found that it would be improper to require a trial on the merits of a case to determine an allocation for purposes of Medicare conditional payment resolution. The *Bradley* Court focused on the strong public policy favoring "expeditious resolution of lawsuits through settlement." According to the court, Medicare's position would have a "chilling effect on settlement." This is so because Medicare's position compels plaintiffs to force their tort claims to trial, burdening the court system. The same argument could be made in the Medicare Set-Aside context for liability settlements that are significantly compromised. Why would an injury victim settle his case if it will all go into a Set-Aside?

There is some basis in CMS' own regulations for a reduction. In 42 C.F.R. 411.47, there is a computation example for workers'

---

247 *Bradley et al v. Sebelius* (11th Cir., No. 09-13765, Sept. 29, 2010).

compensation settlement where there is no allocation in a compromise situation. It is as follows:

> As the result of a work injury, an individual suffered loss of income and incurred medical expenses for which the total workers' compensation payment would have been $24,000 if the case had not been compromised. The medical expenses amounted to $18,000. The workers' compensation carrier made a settlement with the beneficiary under which it paid $8,000 in total. A separate award was made for legal fees. Since the workers' compensation compromise settlement was for one-third of the amount which would have been payable under workers' compensation had the case not been compromised ($8,000/$24,000=1/3), the workers' compensation compromise settlement is considered to have paid for one-third of the total medical expenses (1/3×$18,000=$6,000).

Admittedly, this particular regulation deals with conditional payments and has been flatly rejected by CMS in terms of its use in the context of reducing workers' compensation Medicare Set-Aside arrangements. Nevertheless, this type of analysis makes considerable sense in the context of liability Medicare Set-Asides. Considering CMS has not given any guidance in the liability Medicare Set-Aside area, how can CMS argue it is improper to employ such methods?

So how would you perform a calculation to determine the amount of reduction of a Set-Aside? You could take the approach found in 42 C.F.R. 411.47 or an *Ahlborn* approach. The *Ahlborn* approach would necessitate an estimate of the total value of the claim, which would then be compared to the actual recovery. From there you would determine the percentage of recovery that the settlement represented when compared to the total value of all damages. That type of analysis might look like the following:

$4,000,000 = Total Case Value

$1,000,000 = Settlement

$400,000 = Fees (40 percent fee)

$600,000 = Net

$200,000 = Set-Aside

$30,000 = Reduced Set-Aside (client recovered 15 percent of total damages)

I want to make it very clear that there are no guarantees that CMS would ever approve of either method to reduce a liability Medicare Set-Aside. However, submission to CMS of a liability Set-Aside (and for that matter workers' compensation as well) is voluntary. Accordingly, if one of these methods was utilized and the case was not submitted to CMS for review and approval, I believe CMS would be hard pressed to argue that it was an inappropriate course of action. Given the fact that CMS has ignored questions about how to deal with these issues for liability Medicare Set-Asides and failed to provide any meaningful guidance whatsoever in this area, I believe you could make an estoppel type of argument if CMS ever claimed it was improper.

In conclusion, these trial court orders that have addressed certain issues demonstrate part of the problem lawyers face when dealing with Medicare futures. While the cases are instructive, they are by no means binding on Medicare nor do they have any precedential weight. What they do help with is crafting arguments as to why, in certain cases, there should be a reduced amount set aside or future medicals aren't funded at all. The following chapter is the culmination of chapters 6 through 12 and dives into the issue of what you should be doing within your firm to be totally compliant when settling cases for Medicare beneficiaries.

CHAPTER 13

COMPLIANCE

HOW TO BE TOTALLY MEDICARE COMPLIANT

So, what do lawyers assisting Medicare beneficiaries do given all of the issues I have discussed in the previous chapters? In my opinion, you must put into place a method of screening your files to determine those that involve Medicare beneficiaries or those with a reasonable expectation of becoming a Medicare beneficiary within thirty months. You must contact Medicare and appropriately report the settlement to get a final demand. Then, you audit the final demand and avail yourself of the compromise/waiver process. You must also make sure you identify any potential Part C/MAO liens and resolve those as well.

If you have a Medicare beneficiary or one with a reasonable expectation of becoming one within thirty months as a client, you must determine if future medicals have been funded. If so, then advise the client regarding the legal implications of the MSP related to futures. The easiest way to remember the process once you have identified someone as a Medicare beneficiary or someone with the reasonable expectation is by the acronym "CAD." The "C" stands for consult with competent experts who can help deal with these complicated issues. The "A" stands for advise/

educate the client about the MSP implications related to future medical. The "D" stands for document what you did in relation to the MSP.

If the client decides they don't want an MSA or to set aside anything, a choice they may make, then document the education they received about the issue with them signing an acknowledgment. If they elect to do an MSA analysis, hire a company to do the analysis so they can help you document your file properly and close it compliantly.

In addition, release language is critical when it comes to the question of documentation of considering Medicare's future interests. Release language I have seen prepared by defendant/insurers is typically overbearing. Frequently the language cites regulations that are related to workers' compensation settlements and typically will specifically identify a figure to be set aside. The latter can potentially cause a loss of itemized deductions for the client.

Not only is release language an important consideration, so is the method of calculation of the Set-Aside, potential reduction methodologies, and funding alternatives (lump sum vs. annuity funding). These issues do impact how the release is crafted as well as considerations of whether to submit to CMS for review and approval (which is rarely a good idea). Submission of a liability Set-Aside isn't required and a settlement should never be made contingent upon CMS review and approval. Some regional offices will not review a liability Set-Aside while others will. Since review/approval is voluntary, I typically don't recommend submission given the lack of appeal process should CMS come back with an unfavorable decision. Furthermore, making a settlement contingent upon CMS review/approval could create an impossible contingency if the settlement is in a jurisdiction where the regional office will not review.

Start early and do not let the defendant-insurer control the Medicare compliance process. At the outset of your case, you have to confirm disability eligibility with Social Security and get copies of all insurance as well as government assistance cards. Make sure you understand who is potentially Medicare eligible, such as those who are on SSDI, those turning sixty-five, someone with end-stage renal disease (ESRD), Lou Gehrig's disease (ALS), or a child disabled before age twenty-two with a parent drawing Social Security benefits. Collaborate with the other side regarding what is being reported under MIR. Be active in mandating the proper ICD codes to be included in the release.

All lawyers assisting those on Medicare must be knowledgeable when it comes to dealing with Medicare conditional payments as well as Part C/MAO liens. Medicare beneficiaries must understand the risk of losing their Medicare coverage should they decide to set aside nothing from their personal injury settlement for future Medicare-covered expenses related to the injury. It is about educating the client to make sure they can make an informed decision relative to these issues. Beyond education of the client, the most critical issue becomes how to properly document your file about what was done and why. This part is where the experts come into play. For most practitioners, it is nearly impossible to know all of the nuances and issues that arise with the Medicare Secondary Payer Act. From identifying liens, resolving conditional payments, deciding to set money aside, the creation of the allocation to the release language, and the funding/administration of a Set-Aside, there are issues that can be daunting for even the most well-informed personal injury practitioner. Without proper consultation and guidance, mistakes can lead to unhappy clients, or worse yet, a legal malpractice claim.

The lesson to take away from these chapters on Medicare compliance and the cases described herein, is not to wind up in federal court over these issues. Instead, deal with these issues presettlement strategically. If a client is a Medicare beneficiary, then make sure you know which ICD codes will be reported under the Mandatory Insurer Reporting law and evaluate with the client the possibility of a Set-Aside. Discuss with competent experts the proper steps for MSP compliance. Potentially use the Set-Aside as an element of damages to help improve settlement value. Properly word the release if a Set-Aside is being used to make sure the client doesn't get saddled with inappropriate language or lose itemized deductions. Appropriate planning will avoid a bad outcome or unnecessary trips to federal court.

MEDICARE COMPLIANCE CASE STUDIES

To better understand how to apply the foregoing information, I will illustrate with a few case examples. First, consider a settlement for Jim Doe who is currently forty-six and was injured in a motorcycle accident and lost both of his legs. He worked up until his accident and applied for Social Security Disability (SSDI) after the accident and he was accepted two years ago. He is a current Medicare beneficiary as a result of qualifying for SSDI. You are about to settle his case for $2,000,000 gross and want to make sure you address Medicare compliance issues. In this instance, it makes sense to do a Medicare Set-Aside analysis to document your file regarding what you are doing to deal with the MSP. The settlement will be reported to Medicare under the mandatory insurer reporting requirements which could trigger a future denial of injury-related care. It is ultimately up to the client whether to set aside or not, but your file should be documented about what was done and why. This might be a situation where an argument could be made for a reduced Set-Aside amount based on Ahlborn/Benoit reduction methodologies if the client did want to set aside. It seems likely that here the client would not be recovering their full value of future medical.

Second, consider the case of Jill Doe who was injured as the result of a defective product. Jill was thirty-eight at the time of her incident and suffered a TBI from a tire blowout. She has applied for SSDI but hasn't been accepted yet and is not a current Medicare beneficiary. The defendant is insisting upon an MSA and detailed language in the release. The settlement was for "nuisance value" of $500,000. This is a case where definitively there isn't an MSP compliance issue. The client isn't a Medicare beneficiary and the settlement will not/cannot be reported to Medicare under the mandatory insurer reporting since there is no Medicare entitlement. Here, you should reject the demands by the defendant to set up an MSA and include Medicare language in the release. It isn't appropriate and your client shouldn't acknowledge an obligation that doesn't exist. If the client had applied and been accepted for SSDI, then arguably there could be an MSP compliance issue as they would have a reasonable expectation of Medicare entitlement within thirty months. That category of clients does cause some concern but the settlement still can't be reported to Medicare so there is a very small chance of a denial of care.

Third, consider the case of Bill Smith who was involved in a motor vehicle accident suffering a neck and back injury. Bill was fifty-two at the time of the accident. He was accepted by Social Security as disabled and has been receiving SSDI for the last twenty-three months. He will be Medicare eligible by the time you settle his case for the $100,000 policy limits. The client needs a significant future back surgery which will involve a multilevel fusion. The future medical projection for damages was in excess of $500,000 including that surgical procedure. During litigation, the defense took the position that the neck injuries were preexisting and didn't agree to pay anything for those injuries with the release stating those claims were being released but they were preexisting injuries.

This is a tough one from the MSP compliance standpoint, but it is a common scenario trial lawyers face. Here, even though he isn't currently a Medicare beneficiary, he will be by the time the settlement is consummated, so it will be reported to Medicare. Given the amount of future medicals and the fact that the client will be Medicare eligible when the case settles, MSP compliance issues should be addressed. Here it is very likely that an argument can be made that future medicals weren't funded at all based upon the fact that you have a $100,000 gross settlement and a future medical cost projection of over $500,000. That needs to be properly documented and the client educated about the risk of setting aside nothing by taking the position that future medicals were not funded. Care should be taken to come to an agreement about how to document this file properly for MSP compliance with the defendant. You don't want them to report the neck injury when they do the mandatory insurer reporting so in this case, it might make sense to document in writing with the other side exactly what will be reported.

CHAPTER 14

UNDERSTANDING DUAL ELIGIBILITY

THE INTERPLAY BETWEEN MEDICARE AND MEDICAID

In separate previous chapters, I have discussed the implications for settlement when representing someone who was either on Medicaid or Medicare. Some individuals are "dual eligible" meaning they qualify for both Medicaid and Medicare. In certain cases, a Medicare Set-Aside/Special Needs Trust or pooled trust subaccount may be necessary to preserve the client's dual eligibility. As discussed previously, Medicare Set-Asides are a device used to preserve future Medicare eligibility. Currently, the use of Set-Asides in liability settlements is at best a grey area. However, in an abundance of caution, it may be prudent to consider setting one up when the injury victim is a Medicare beneficiary or reasonably expected to become Medicare eligible within thirty months. A Special Needs Trust or pooled Special Needs Trust is appropriate for clients receiving Supplemental Security Income (SSI) and/or Medicaid benefits. Federal law allows creation of either an SNT or pooled Special Needs Trust to preserve eligibility for needs-based benefits, such as SSI and Medicaid, post-settlement of a personal injury claim.

This chapter will explore the concept of dual eligibility. I will discuss exactly what it is and how Medicaid coordinates with Medicare for those that are dual eligible. Finally, I will detail the techniques to preserve Medicaid and Medicare for those that have dual eligibility.

DUAL ELIGIBILITY

Dual eligibility is not extremely common, but there is a subset of the injury population who will be dual eligible. Understanding who qualifies for both Medicaid and Medicare is vitally important for the personal injury practitioner to ensure that the injury victim's benefits are adequately protected. By CMS' definition, dual eligible clients are those who qualify for Medicare Part A and/or Part B and also qualify for Medicaid programs as well. Medicare coverage can be obtained prior to age sixty-five if an injury victim qualifies for Social Security Disability. It takes a total of thirty months for someone who is disabled to qualify for Medicare (Medicare coverage begins twenty-four months after the first SSDI check is received, which takes five months, and includes the month of receipt, so plus one month).

Medicare Part A provides inpatient hospital care, acute hospital care, and limited nursing home care. Physician care in the hospital is also covered by part A. There are no premiums to be paid for Medicare Part A if an individual has enough work credits ("qualifying quarters"). However, one can pay for the coverage if they do not have sufficient work credits. Medicare Part B, by contrast, covers outpatient medical services, physician services outside the hospital, and other miscellaneous services not covered by Part A. Medicare Part B has a monthly premium associated with it, which is often deducted from the recipient's Social Security check and the premiums for the Part B coverage increases for those with more income.

Some Medicare beneficiaries have so little income or assets that they also qualify for state programs through Medicaid that pay for certain out-of-pocket expenses not covered by the Medicare program. There are several different programs that injury victims who qualify for Medicaid may be entitled to that help with expenses not covered by Medicare. In addition, there are services that Medicare does not pay for that can be covered by state Medicaid programs. For example, Medicare does not cover nursing home care beyond one hundred days yet Medicaid does, if one qualifies, cover that care.

The programs that cover out-of-pocket expenses provide limited Medicaid benefits to those who qualify. Through these programs, Medicaid will pay Medicare premiums, copayments and deductibles within prescribed limits. There are two different programs. First, is Qualified Medicare Beneficiaries (QMB). The QMB program pays for the recipient's Medicare premiums (Parts A and B), Medicare deductibles, and Medicare coinsurance within the prescribed limits. QMB recipients also automatically qualify for extra help with the Medicare Part D prescription drug plan costs. The income and asset caps are higher[248] than the normal SSI/Medicaid qualification limits. Second is Special Low-Income Medicare Beneficiary (SLMB). The SLMB program pays for Medicare premiums for Part B Medicare benefits. SLMB recipients automatically qualify for extra help with Medicare Part D prescription drug plan costs. Again, the income and asset caps are higher[249] than the normal SSI/Medicaid qualification limits.

The Centers for Medicare and Medicaid Services (CMS) provides

---

248 Resources must be at or below twice the standard allowed under the Supplemental Security Income (SSI) program and income at or below 100 percent of the federal poverty level.

249 Resources must be at or below twice the standard allowed under the SSI program and income exceeding the QMB level, but less than 120 percent of the federal poverty level.

the following chart on their website of available benefits for those with dual eligibility:

TYPE OF MEDICAID BENEFIT

DUAL ELIGIBLE CATEGORY	PART A PREMIUM	PART B PREMIUM	MEDICARE COST-SHARING	FULL MEDICAID BENEFITS
MEDICAID ONLY	No	Yes	No	Yes
QMB	Yes	Yes	Yes	No
QMB PLUS	Yes	Yes	Yes	Yes
SLMB	No	Yes	No	No
SLMB PLUS	No	Yes	No	Yes
QI	No	Yes	No	No
QDWI	Yes	No	No	No

According to CMS, the "plus" categories were "created when Congress changed eligibility criteria for QMBs and SLMBs to eliminate the requirement that QMBs and SLMBs could not otherwise qualify for Medicaid." QDWI stands for Qualified Disabled and Working Individual, which is someone who lost Medicare Part A coverage after returning to work who may enroll in and purchase Medicare Part A. There are income and asset caps[250] for this program similar to other programs.

PRESERVATION OF PUBLIC BENEFITS FOR THOSE WHO ARE DUAL ELIGIBLE

For injury victims who are Medicare eligible or reasonably likely to be within thirty months, a trial lawyer must carefully consider compliance with the Medicare Secondary Payer Act (MSP). For

---

250 Resources must not exceed twice the SSI limit and must have income of 200 percent of federal poverty level or less. QDWIs must not be otherwise eligible for Medicaid benefits.

those injury victims receiving needs-based benefits such as SSI and Medicaid, planning is necessary to preserve those benefits. If you represent a client who is a Medicaid and Medicare recipient, extra planning may be necessary. If it is determined that a Medicare Set-Aside is appropriate, it raises some issues with continued Medicaid eligibility. A Medicare Set-Aside account is considered an available resource for purposes of needs-based benefits such as SSI/Medicaid. If the Medicare Set-Aside account is not set up inside a Special Needs Trust, the client will lose Medicaid/SSI eligibility. Therefore, in order for someone with dual eligibility to maintain their Medicaid/SSI benefits, the MSA must be put inside a Special Needs Trust. In this instance you would have a hybrid trust which addresses both Medicaid and Medicare. It is a complicated planning tool but one that is essential when you have those with dual eligibility.

DUAL ELIGIBILITY CASE STUDY

To better understand how to apply the foregoing information, I will illustrate with a case example. Suppose you represent an injury victim, Mitch Smith, who was hit by a car while crossing a street in a pedestrian crosswalk. At the time of the accident, Mitch was sixty-two years old and a low-wage earner but had paid enough into the system to be fully insured. When he got hit, he had very few assets. After the accident, he qualified for and started to receive SSDI and consequently Medicare. He also qualified for the QMB Medicaid program. The settlement you have secured is for the policy limits of $500,000. Mr. Smith suffered primarily lower extremity orthopedic injuries and a slight TBI. It is anticipated he may need one future surgery to correct some of the damage done to his right knee. Because he is older and due to his injuries, he will never work again. He needs every penny of government assistance he gets. Medicare is primary but

Medicaid pays for what Medicare does not cover so it is comprehensive coverage.

In this scenario, you need to worry about both a Medicare Set-Aside and a Special Needs Trust to preserve those precious benefits. Here, it is recommended that you do the analysis to set up a Medicare Set-Aside. However, that only deals with the Medicare preservation. For Medicaid planning purposes, he would need both an MSA/SNT and an SNT. So, the MSA that is to be created would be held inside of an SNT to avoid it being a countable resource. This planning will make sure that the client not only has the benefit of Medicaid but also Medicare as well.

CHAPTER 15

ERISA LIEN RESOLUTION

Although a deep dive into ERISA law and liens is beyond the scope of this book, this chapter will give you an overview and a starting point. The Employee Retirement Income Security Act was passed by Congress and signed into law by President Ford in 1974.[251] According to the US Department of Labor, ERISA "protects the interests of employee benefit plan participants and their beneficiaries. It requires plan sponsors to provide plan information to participants. It establishes standards of conduct for plan managers and other fiduciaries. It establishes enforcement provisions to ensure that plan funds are protected and that qualifying participants receive their benefits, even if a company goes bankrupt." Many would not agree with that statement when it comes to actually protecting plan participants as it relates to resolution of ERISA liens, but that is the stated purpose.

ERISA governs nearly all employer health plans. The primary exceptions are government employer plans governed by FEHBA and state government or church plans which are governed by state law. Most, if not all, ERISA health insurance plans state that injuries caused by a liable third party are not a covered expense

---

251 29 U.S.C. 1001, et seq.

and require reimbursement when a plan pays for injury-related medical expenses (often referred to as subrogation clauses). ERISA provides that health plans which qualify under its provisions can bring a civil action under section 502(a)(3) to obtain equitable relief to enforce the terms of the plan. Appropriate equitable relief is really the only enforcement mechanism an ERISA plan can utilize to address its reimbursement rights contained in the plan. While that all may sound simple, ERISA is a "compressive and reticulated statute" which means that the law on this subject is quite complicated.[252] So the Supreme Court has clarified exactly what is appropriate equitable relief under ERISA over the last twenty years.

Starting in 2006, the United States Supreme Court began to clarify and articulate just how powerful a "self-funded" ERISA plan's recovery rights are under federal law. In 2006, the Supreme Court issued its opinion *Sereboff*.[253] In that decision, the Supreme Court found generally that reimbursement provisions asserted by ERISA group medical plans were enforceable under the ERISA statute and qualified as equitable relief under the ERISA provisions.[254] Prior to *Sereboff*, there was disagreement among federal courts about whether an ERISA plan could even enforce its repayment provisions. Post *Sereboff*, an ERISA qualifying plan's contractual provisions for repayment can be enforced via equitable principles under section 502(a)(3) by filing an action for an equitable lien or for constructive trust.[255]

In 2013, the *McCutchen* case was decided by the Supreme

---

252 *Great-West v. Knudson*, 534 U.S. 204, 209 (2002).

253 *Sereboff v. Mid Atlantic Medical Servs., Inc.* 547 U.S. 356 (2006).

254 *Id.*

255 *Id.*

Court.[256] After the *Sereboff* decision was issued, most lawyers understood that to defeat reimbursement actions under ERISA it depended on the strength of equitable defenses/arguments like "made whole" and "common fund." *McCutchen* took on the issue of whether those doctrines could prevent an ERISA plan from enforcing its recovery rights. The exact question as framed by the Supreme Court was "[w]hether the Third Circuit correctly held—in conflict with the Fifth, Seventh, Eighth, Eleventh, and D.C. Circuits—that ERISA Section 502(a)(3) authorizes courts to use equitable principles to rewrite contractual language and refuse to order participants to reimburse their plan for benefits paid, even where the plan's terms give it an absolute right to full reimbursement." At the time, there was a split of the federal circuits on the question of whether notions of fairness (equitable defenses) could override an ERISA medical plan's reimbursement provisions. The *McCutchen* Court reversed the Third Circuit and held that in a section 502(a)(3) action based on an equitable lien by agreement, the ERISA plan's terms govern. "Neither general unjust enrichment principles nor specific doctrines reflecting those principles—such as the double-recovery or common-fund rules invoked by McCutchen—can override the applicable contract."

Post *McCutchen*, the lesson to savvy plans is to word your master plan in such a way to prevent any and all equitable defenses by disavowing "made whole" and "common fund." This is so since the root of the holding in *McCutchen* was that the written terms of the ERISA plan win the day over any possible equitable defenses. In its now infamous "McCutchen memo," Rawlings stated that "it is now undisputed throughout the entire nation that general principles of unjust enrichment and equitable doctrines 'reflect-

---

256 *U.S. Airways, Inc. v. McCutchen*, 133 S.Ct. 1537 (2013).

ing those principles' cannot override an applicable ERISA plan contract." Obviously the *McCutchen* decision is important and a tough pill to swallow for the plaintiff who makes a recovery and then must reimburse an ERISA plan. While it is important, there are still many ways to get leverage and reduce ERISA plan liens, but you must know the pressure points to use. You also must realize who you are fighting. In most instances, it isn't the plans but instead their recovery vendors like Rawlings, Conduent, Trover, among many others. These are big, powerful companies who employ thousands in large, beautiful office buildings with the single goal of riding the coattails of the trial lawyer's hard work to get reimbursement for the plan. They are paid based on what they recover so there is plenty of incentive for the industry players to work hard against the plaintiff.

In fighting plans, the first and most important question is whether the plan is self-funded or not. A self-funded plan is funded by contributions from the employer and employee. If it is self-funded, then ERISA preempts state law and you are left with fighting an uphill battle under *McCutchen*. If it is fully insured, then the ERISA plan is subject to state law subrogation statutes or general equitable principles under common law. These are plans which are funded by purchased insurance coverage. How do you determine the funding status? The safest way is by reviewing the Summary Plan Description (SPD) and the Master Plan. How do you get those documents? Simply put, you make a written request to the ERISA plan administrator under 29 U.S.C. §1024(b) (4). Under 1024(b)(4), an ERISA plan administrator must provide, upon request by a participant or beneficiary, a copy of the summary plan description, annual report, "bargaining agreement, trust agreement, contract, or other instruments under which the plan is established or operated." The request must go to the plan itself, not the plan administrator (TPA) or its recovery contractor (i.e., Rawlings, Optum, Conduent, etc.). If the plan administrator does not comply within thirty days, 29 U.S.C. §1132(c)(1)(b) establishes a $100 per day penalty for failure to comply. Further, 29 U.S.C. §2575.502c-1 allows for this penalty to be increased to $110 per day. There are plenty of cases out there where federal courts have imposed penalties upon a plan administrator for failing to comply.[257]

In order to combat ERISA plan recovery attempts, the information received from the 1024(b)(4) request is critical. You want to evaluate the strength of the plan's claim based on the language in the plan. The 1024(b)(4) request arms you with the proper information to do so. This allows you to make the appropriate arguments for reduction. What you are looking for is abrogation of "common fund" and "made whole" primarily. If those equitable principles have not been abrogated, there are strong arguments for reduction. In addition, when the plan administrator fails to comply with the request, and they often do, penalties will begin to accrue. Once penalties have accrued, you have more leverage to negotiate with the ERISA recovery contractor for a reduced lien amount.

To sum up, when evaluating an ERISA plan's right of recovery, it is important to first determine if it is in fact a plan covered by ERISA

---

257 See generally in the Second Circuit, the cases are *McDonald v. Pension Plan of the Nysa-Ila Pension Trust Fund*, 320 F.3d 151, 163 (2d Cir. 2002) ($15/day for 71 days; $1,065 total); in the Third Circuit, *Gorini v. AMP*, Inc., 94 Fed. Appx. 913, 916 (3d Cir. April 16, 2004)(award of $160,780 for an unnamed amount of time); in the Fourth Circuit, *Faircloth v. Lundy Packing Co.*, 91 F.3d 648, 659 (4th Cir. 1996)($2500 for each of three plaintiffs for a delay of about 90 days); in the Seventh Circuit, *Blazejewski v. Gibson*, 1999 U.S. Dist. LEXIS 18028 at 14 (N.D. Ill. 1999)($10/day for about 400 days); in the Eighth Circuit, *Keogan v. Towers*, 2003 U.S. Dist. LEXIS 7999 at 34 (D. Minn. 2003) ($100/day for 649 days; $64,900 total); in the Ninth Circuit, *Advisory Comm. for Stock Ownership & Trust for Employees of Montana Bancsystem, Inc. v. Kuhn*, 1996 U.S. App. LEXIS 2273 at 22-23 (9th Cir. 1996) ($33/day for 586 days; total of 19,338); in the Tenth Circuit, *Dehner v. Kansas City S. Indus., Inc.*, 713 F. Supp. 1397, 1402 (D. Kan. 1989)($20/day for 84 days; $1680 total); in the Eleventh Circuit, *Curry v. Contract Fabricators, Inc. Profit Sharing Plan*, 891 F.2d 842, 848 (11th Cir. 1990) ($3/ day for 240 days; $800 total).

and then secondly if it is a self-funded plan. The *McCutchen* decision has given ERISA self-funded plans strong recovery rights under federal law. Since under that decision plan language is vitally important, using a 1024(b)(4) request to get plan documents is an important tool to properly evaluate the strength of a reimbursement claim. In addition, failure to comply with this information request provides for penalties that can be leveraged to get the lien resolved.

CHAPTER 16

FEHBA/MILITARY LIEN RESOLUTION

In this chapter, you will get an overview of common issues that arise when representing clients who have healthcare coverage by virtue of their employment with the federal government or military service. For federal workers, they get their coverage through specialized plans provided under federal law. Military service members and their dependents are covered through different programs based upon their service. When settling cases for these classes of clients, it is important to understand the recovery rights of government health plans which are summarized below. Since this area is not succinct, below is a summary of salient points so that you can issue spot.

FEHBA

The Federal Employees Health Benefits program provides health insurance coverage to federal employees, retirees, and their survivors. Federal law, found at 5 U.S.C. § 8901 et seq. (Federal Employees Health Benefits Act or FEHBA), governs these programs, which provide benefits to millions of federal workers and their dependents. FEHBA authorizes the Office of Personnel Management (OPM) to enter into contracts with private insurance carriers to administer FEHB plans. OPM's contracts have traditionally required the private insurance carriers to pursue subrogation and reimbursement. According to the Supreme Court, "FEHBA expressly 'preempt[s] any state or local law' that would prevent enforcement of 'the terms of any contract' between OPM and a carrier which 'relate to the nature, provision, or extent of coverage or benefits (including payments with respect to benefits).' Id. § 8902(m)(l)." "In a 2015 regulation, OPM codified its longstanding position that FEHBA-contract provisions requiring carriers to seek subrogation or reimbursement 'relate to...benefits' and 'payments with respect to benefits,' and therefore FEHBA preempts state laws that purport to prevent FEHBA insurance carriers from pursuing subrogation and reimbursement recoveries. 5 C.F.R. § 890.106(h)."

A 2017 United States Supreme Court decision is the seminal case on FEHBA plans and their recovery rights from personal injury settlements. In *Coventry Healthcare of Missouri Inc. v. Nevils*,[258] the court was asked to decide whether FEHBA preempts state laws that prevent these plans from seeking subrogation or reimbursement pursuant to FEHBA contracts and whether FEHBA's express-preemption clause (5 U.S.C. § 8902(m)(l)) violates the Supremacy Clause. The case came to the Supreme Court from the Missouri Supreme Court, which interpreted FEHBA not to preempt state law and finding that Section 8902 violated the Supremacy Clause of the US Constitution. The United States Supreme Court unanimously reversed the holding of the Missouri Supreme Court because "contractual subrogation and reimbursement prescriptions plainly 'relate to...payments with respect to benefits,' §8902(m)(1), they override state laws barring subrogation and reimbursement" and "[t]he regime Congress enacted is compatible with the Supremacy Clause."[259]

---

258 *Coventry Health Care of Missouri, Inc. V. Nevils*, 137 S. Ct. 1190, 197 L. Ed. 2d 572, 581 US _ (2017).

259 *Id.*

Nevils has empowered FEHBA plans to demand full reimbursement when a settlement occurs. With the holding that FEHBA preempts state law and that such preemption is constitutionally permissible, *Nevils* has ended future disputes between private litigants and FEHBA carriers over whether state subrogation laws limited their recovery rights. Now, it is very clear that federal preemption applies, and state law provisions have no impact on the arguments to reduce a FEHBA lien. Unfortunately, this makes FEHBA liens similar to ERISA plan liens in that they have very powerful recovery rights under federal law that completely preempt state law. The good news is that most FEHBA plans do not have as draconian recovery provisions as ERISA plans, which does mean there is the possibility of a reasonable reduction, but it is far more difficult post-*Nevils*. As with most insurance plans, the first step in attempting to reduce the lien is reviewing the FEHBA plan's language that governs the client's healthcare coverage with the government. This information is available on the OPM's website.[260]

MILITARY LIENS

While much more attention is paid to Medicare, ERISA, and other lien types, federal reimbursement rights of military programs should be on a trial lawyer's radar. With a rise in those serving in the US military abroad leaving their families at home, claims involving these plans are rising. There are three different types of coverages available to those in the military and their dependents/ survivors. First, the Veterans Health Administration delivers healthcare insurance to eligible and enrolled veterans encompassing both inpatient and outpatient services at their facilities. Second, ChampVA is health insurance provided through the

---

260 See https://www.opm.gov/healthcare-insurance/healthcare/plan-information/plans/.

Civilian Health and Medical Program of the Department of Veteran Affairs for the spouse or child of a veteran with disabilities or a veteran who has died. Third, Tricare is the Department of Defense's healthcare program for active-duty and retired service members and their families. The legal starting point for reimbursement claims when it comes to the military is the Federal Medical Care Recovery Act (FMCRA). It is found at 42 U.S.C. §§ 2651-2653 and provides the federal government with the right to recover the medical expenses incurred for medical care of an injured beneficiary when there is a liable third party. Under this act, the United States has a right to recover the reasonable value of the care and treatment from the person(s) responsible for the injury. It is noteworthy that there really is no "military lien" and instead, a direct cause of action against the third party under FMCRA. In addition, 10 U.S.C. §1095 is the basis upon which the government relies to recover from liable third parties and requires the beneficiary to protect its interests. The government, through these military healthcare programs, demands that plaintiff attorneys sign protection agreements to acknowledge the claim and protect the interests of the federal government. Signing these types of agreements is generally not advisable for the reasons I outline below. Accordingly, health insurance coverage under the Veterans' Administration (VA), ChampVA, and Tricare all have recovery rights under FMCRA and other provisions of the federal law.

The VA's recovery rights come from 38 U.S.C. § 1729 and FMCRA (42 U.S.C. §§2651–2653) and allows them to, after rendering treatment, pursue recovery provided that is connected to a compensable third-party claim. Under federal law, the VA has both an independent right of recovery from responsible third parties and a right of subrogation, assignment, and ability to intervene or join a beneficiary's claim. According to § 1729 of the United

States Code, "the United States has the right to recover or collect reasonable charges for such care or services (as determined by the Secretary) from a third party to the extent that the veteran (or the provider of the care or services) would be eligible to receive payment for such care or services from such third party if the care or services had not been furnished by a department or agency of the United States." When care is received at a military or VA facility, there can be significant delays in resolving their claim because you must request that a bill be generated. These requests can take sixty days or more to process. There are forms for this kind of request included on the VA's website.[261] If you want to request a compromise or waiver of a VA subrogation claim, you must provide the amount of settlement, attorney's fees and costs, other medical claims and reductions, and overall policy limits available. There are three tiers of review for compromise/waiver requests. Tier one is the Revenue Law Group who must approve requests for a compromise or waiver on claims between $1 and $300,000. Tier two is the DOJ who must approve requests for a compromise or waiver on claims between $300,000 and one million dollars.[262] Tier three is the Office of the Attorney General who must approve all requests for a compromise or waiver on claims greater than one million dollars.[263]

Tricare is similar to the VA as its recovery rights are governed by the same federal law provisions as the VA (38 U.S.C. §1729 and 42 U.S.C. §§2651–2653) along with 32 C.F.R. §199.12. And like the VA, Tricare also has both a right of subrogation and an independent right of recovery from responsible third parties. While Tricare doesn't require Set-Asides, Section 199.12 states "[n]o TriCare-

---

261 https://www.va.gov/OGC/Collections.asp.

262 *Id.*

263 *Id.*

related claim will be settled, compromised or waived without full consideration being given to the possible future medical payment aspects of the individual case." So, these regulations do allow Tricare to include future medical related to the personal injury claim as part of their recovery claim. Tricare claims are generally resolved through the JAG office where the military serviceman is posted. While "made whole" and "common fund" doesn't apply to subrogation claims under FMCRA, reductions may be granted when there is an undue burden placed upon the injured party.

Two problematic issues come up with military reimbursement claims. The first issue relates to attorney fees and Tricare. The military's official position is stated in their form protection agreement which states in pertinent part that "Title 5, United States Code, Section 3106, prohibits the payment of a fee for representing the Government." It goes on to state, "[f]urther, as the claim of the Government is an independent cause of action rather than a lien on any settlement or judgment obtained by the injured party, any contingent fee arrangement with the injured party applies solely to the client's claim and not to the Government's portion of the recovery." In resolving a reimbursement claim with the military, one will have to navigate the issue of fees and costs as applied to the whole settlement versus the amount less the "Government's portion of the recovery." Arguably, you can take your whole fee if you refuse to sign the protection agreement, but you will get pushback from the JAG officer you will be dealing with to resolve the military's claim when requesting a compromise or waiver of the military's claim.

The second issue is whether the military has a claim against first-party auto insurance policies. The question of whether the military has a right to recover its claim for medical expenses against UM is determined by the UM policy's language. FMCRA does not directly provide the government with a right to recover its claim against first-party insurance proceeds. This issue was addressed in *Government Employees Ins. Co. v. Andujar*[264] which arguably, properly held that the US military didn't have a reimbursement claim directly against UM proceeds under FMCRA. Under FMCRA, as discussed above, the government's claim is only against the tortfeasor. In *Andujar*, neither the injured party or their UM insurer were considered the tortfeasor, and accordingly, there was no right to recover from the UM auto policy proceeds. It is also important to note that in *Andujar*, there was specific policy language in the automobile insurance contract that stated the government was not covered by the policy. Accordingly, the result can be different where the automobile policy provisions protect the government or where applicable, state law provides that protection. So, an important part of the analysis when dealing with a reimbursement claim by the military is the express language of the automobile policy. If the government can be considered a third-party beneficiary or insured under the automobile policy, then they may have a right to reimbursement. This is precisely what the *Andujar* decision turned on.

In the end, FEHBA plans have very strong recovery rights under the *Nevils* case. FEHBA completely preempts state subrogation laws so arguments for reduction must be made based on the policy language. Fortunately, most FEHBA plans aren't as punitive as ERISA plans, so often there are reductions available. Military liens are governed by the Federal Medical Care Recovery Act, which provides the federal government with the right to recover the medical expenses incurred for medical care of an injured beneficiary when there is a liable third party. There

---

264 773 F. Supp 282 (D. Kan. 1991).

are different issues that arise when it comes to Tricare and for example attorney fees reduction and whether the military has reimbursement rights from first-party recoveries.

CHAPTER 17

ADVANCED SETTLEMENT PLANNING TECHNIQUES AND REAL-WORLD APPLICATION

This chapter examines the intersection of the complicated issues around government benefit preservation and what to do with the financial recovery for a disabled injury victim. In the confusing landscape of public benefits and planning issues that arise today for trial lawyers when settling catastrophic injury cases, finding your way can be a daunting task. Many questions come up, such as should the client seek SSDI benefits and become Medicare eligible? Doesn't that trigger the need for a Medicare Set-Aside? What if the client is receiving needs-based benefits such as Medicaid and/or SSI? Is coverage under the Affordable Care Act (ACA)[265] a better or even an available option? How should the recovery be managed from a financial perspective? Is a trust appropriate? Should a structured settlement be considered? There are no easy answers to these questions. In the paragraphs that follow, you will find useful information related to these issues that will give

---

265 Patient Protection and Affordable Care Act, 42 U.S.C. § 18001 et seq. (2010).

trial lawyers the ability to spot issues when settling a case for a catastrophically injured client.

Let's use a real-world example to identify the issues. Take Jan Smith who was the victim of medical malpractice at a hospital. Jan was in her early forties when she decided to have elective surgery on her back for degenerative disc disease. During the surgery, a problem developed while being intubated and the procedure was cancelled. Mrs. Smith was moved to the ICU and no neurologic monitoring was performed that evening after being moved from the surgical suite. The next morning, Mrs. Smith was found to be quadriparetic. Unfortunately for Mrs. Smith, her condition was irreversible. Suit was brought against multiple defendants with a significant seven-figure recovery secured. Mrs. Smith and her family had Medicaid coverage and SSI. She had also applied for SSDI. At the time of settlement, there was no Medicare eligibility, since she had not been approved for SSDI and she wasn't sixty-five. How do you protect the client's eligibility for public benefits? Is that the right thing to do? Should ACA coverage be considered? What about protection of the monies recovered on Mrs. Smith's behalf? Should a trust be created? What about structured settlements? Let's explore these questions further.

PUBLIC BENEFITS VERSUS ACA COVERAGE

As a starting point, the first question is, does it make sense for Mrs. Smith to give up her needs-based benefits completely by taking the settlement in a lump sum and becoming privately insured through coverage under the Affordable Care Act? This isn't a question that can be answered with a simple yes or no. There are multiple considerations before deciding to eschew coverage afforded by Medicaid and Medicare along with the needs-based Social Security benefit, SSI. First is whether the

ACA coverage will be around for the long term. Will it be repealed at some point? Will portions of it be repealed making it a nonviable option? Second, does the case involve needs that aren't provided for by the Affordable Care Act coverage such as in-home, skilled attendant care or long-term facility care? These services can be very costly and may be covered by Medicaid in many states but are not covered by ACA plans. In Mrs. Smith's case, she will have a significant amount of attendant care needs that can be covered by certain Medicaid programs available in her home state but not by the ACA. So, does that mean she shouldn't apply for ACA coverage? Should she create a Special Needs Trust to protect Medicaid and SSI? The answer lies in an analysis of the costs of the plans available under the ACA and the amount of spendable income that results if a Special Needs Trust is utilized.

According to a 2013 article authored by Kevin Urbatsch and Scott MacDonald entitled "The Affordable Care and Settlement Planning"[266] the numbers favor combining ACA coverage with a Special Needs Trust. The following chart illustrates the financial benefits of combining an SNT with ACA coverage in California.

---

266 The Affordable Care Act and Settlement Planning, Kevin Urbatsch & Scott MacDonald, *Plaintiff* magazine (December 2013).

PLANNING PROJECTIONS (FORTY-YEAR-OLD FEMALE)

SETTLEMENT NET ASSET LEVEL =>	$100 K	$396 K	$500 K	$1 M	$2.868 M
	NET SPENDABLE INCOME—ANNUAL AMOUNT [U][267]				
SNT ONLY [V][268]	$12,610	$23,751	$22,208	$33,484	$67,500
NO SNT, BUY ACA INSURANCE [W][269]	EM[270]	EM	$11,196	$15,794	$67,504
SNT WITH ACA SUPPLEMENTAL [W]	EM	EM	$17,700	$20,684	$53,766
NO SNT, EXPANDED MEDI-CAL	$3,614	$14,291	NQ[271]	NQ	NQ
INCOME PERCENT OF FEDERAL POVERTY LIMIT [X][272]	34.80%	138% [y][273]	174.06%	348.13%	600.70%
AVERAGE ANNUAL ACA PREMIUM (NET SUBSIDY) [Z][274]	$0	$0	$4,508	$12,800	$15,552
AVERAGE MONTHLY ACA PREMIUM (NET SUBSIDY)	$0	$0	$376	$1,067	$1,296

Source: Merrill Lynch Wealth Management Analysis through the Wealth Outlook Program, May 2013.

---

267 *Id.* (**u:** After-tax spendable income, net of premium or SNT expenses, assuming 2.5 percent COLA through actuarial life expectancy of the beneficiary).

268 *Id.* (**v:** Net Spendable Income for SNT options has been reduced by $3,000 expense to establish the SNT and 1 percent annual administrative expenses.).

269 *Id.* (**w:** Net Spendable Income for ACA options has been reduced by average annual premium and maximum annual out-of-pocket expenses for the respective income level (based on percent of FPL)).

270 *Id.* (**EM:** Qualifies for the Expanded Medi-Cal Program).

271 *Id.* (**NQ:** Not Qualified for Expanded Medi-Cal Program).

272 *Id.* (**x:** Assumes 4 percent annual taxable income based on the settlement net asset level).

273 *Id.* (**y:** Maximum annual income level to qualify for the Expanded Medi-Cal Program is 133 percent of the federal poverty limit ($15,282) plus 5% ($11,490 * .05% = $574.50) any income disregard = $15,856 for 2013).

274 *Id.* (**z:** Average of highest premium rate for that income level across the 19 California regions. Amount shown is beneficiary's cost after federal subsidy).

As the chart demonstrates, there can be some distinct advantages from a financial perspective to utilizing ACA coverage but also keeping Medicaid/SSI eligibility. While that is true, it also is true that a Special Needs Trust, which would preserve Medicaid and SSI, places many restrictions on how settlement monies may be used. Accordingly, it isn't a decision that should be made just for financial reasons. A careful analysis of all the issues is necessary. In the case of Mrs. Smith, other considerations outweighed the use of a Special Needs Trust. She and her family didn't want the restrictions that come with the SNT. Since monies were allocated to her spouse and their children, all of the family's assets disqualified her for needs-based benefits.

Even though she was currently ineligible for needs-based benefits, that didn't mean she could never become eligible again in the future. Mrs. Smith might have need for means-tested benefits such as Medicaid/SSI in the future and could become a Medicare beneficiary at some point as well, and therefore a trust with provisions that would protect these benefits was created. The trust had provisions that would allow the trustee to move money into a "special needs sub-trust" and a "Medicare Set-Aside sub-trust." The Set-Aside sub-trust was contained within the "special needs sub-trust" so that in the event the client was "dual eligible," the Set-Aside wouldn't cause an eligibility problem for needs-based benefits. Also, let's now make the assumption that the ACA coverage isn't an option or perhaps might not be around well into the future. What are the types of benefits an injury victim should be concerned about preserving and what are the techniques used to preserve them?

PUBLIC ASSISTANCE PROGRAM ANALYSIS

Because Mrs. Smith is eligible for Medicaid and SSI as well as having applied for SSDI, further explanation of these benefits makes sense to adequately understand the issues involved in planning for her recovery. There are two primary public benefit programs that are available to those who are injured and disabled. The first is the Medicaid program and the intertwined Supplemental Security Income benefit (SSI). The second is the Medicare program and the related Social Security Disability Income/Retirement benefit (SSDI). Both programs can be adversely impacted by an injury victim's receipt of a personal injury recovery. As discussed in previous chapters, understanding the basics of these programs and their differences is imperative to protecting the client's eligibility for these benefits. So how do we protect Mrs. Smith's current and potential future benefits?

PLANNING TECHNIQUES FOR KEEPING MRS. SMITH ELIGIBLE FOR MEDICAID/SSI

Since Mrs. Smith receives Medicaid/SSI, an SNT can be created to hold the recovery and preserve public benefit eligibility since assets held within a Special Needs Trust are not a countable resource for purposes of Medicaid or SSI eligibility. The creation of a Special Needs Trust is authorized by federal law.[275] Trusts commonly referred to as (d)(4)(a) Special Needs Trusts, named after the federal code section that authorizes their creation, are for those under the age of sixty-five.[276] However, another type of trust is authorized under the federal law with no age restriction and it is called a pooled trust, commonly referred to as a (d)(4) (c) trust.[277]

---

275 42 U.S.C. §1396p (d)(4).

276 42 U.S.C. §1396p (d)(4)(A).

277 42 U.S.C. §1396p (d)(4)(C).

For a more thorough explanation of Special Needs Trusts, refer to page 17. To summarize, the 1396p[278] provisions in the United States Code govern the creation and requirements for such trusts. First and foremost, a client must be disabled in order to create a SNT.[279] There are two primary types of trusts that may be created to hold a personal injury recovery each with its own requirements and restrictions. First is the (d)(4)(A)[280] Special Needs Trust which can be established only for those who are disabled and are under age sixty-five. This trust is established with the personal injury victim's recovery and is established for the victim's own benefit. It can only be established by a parent, grandparent, guardian, or court order. The injury victim can't create it on his or her own. Second is a (d)(4)(C)[281] trust typically called a pooled trust that may be established with the disabled victim's funds without regard to age. A pooled trust can be established by the injury victim unlike a (d)(4)(A).

PLANNING TECHNIQUES FOR MAKING SURE MRS. SMITH WILL NOT LOSE MEDICARE COVERAGE IN THE FUTURE

Mrs. Smith has applied for SSDI which means technically, according to CMS guidance, she has a "reasonable expectation of becoming a Medicare beneficiary within thirty months." A client who is a current Medicare beneficiary or is reasonably expected to become one within thirty months should concern every trial lawyer because of the implications of the Medicare Secondary Payer Act (MSP). Under the MSP, Medicare isn't supposed to pay for future medical expenses covered by a liability

---

278 42 U.S.C. §1396p.

279 To be considered disabled for purposes of creating an SNT, the SNT beneficiary must meet the definition of disability for SSDI found at 42 U.S.C. §1382c.

280 42 U.S.C. §1396p (d)(4)(A).

281 42 U.S.C. §1396p (d)(4)(C).

or workers' compensation settlement, judgment, or award. CMS recommends that injury victims set aside a sufficient amount to cover future medical expenses that are Medicare covered. CMS' recommended way to protect an injury victim's future Medicare benefit eligibility is establishment of a Medicare Set-Aside (MSA) to pay for injury-related care until exhaustion.

In certain cases, a Medicare Set-Aside may be advisable in order to preserve future eligibility for Medicare coverage. A Medicare Set-Aside allows an injury victim to preserve Medicare benefits by setting aside a portion of the settlement money in a segregated account to pay for future Medicare-covered healthcare. The funds in the Set-Aside can only be used for Medicare-covered expenses for the client's injury-related care. Once the Set-Aside account is exhausted, the client gets full Medicare coverage without Medicare ever looking to their remaining settlement dollars to provide for any Medicare-covered healthcare. In certain circumstances, Medicare approves the amount to be set aside in writing and agrees to be responsible for all future expenses once the Set-Aside funds are depleted.

DUAL ELIGIBILITY: THE INTERSECTION OF MEDICARE AND MEDICAID—SNT/MSA

Since Mrs. Smith is potentially a Medicaid and Medicare recipient, extra planning is in order. If it is determined that a Medicare Set-Aside is appropriate or needed in the future, it raises some issues with continued Medicaid eligibility. A Medicare Set-Aside account is considered an available resource for purposes of needs-based benefits such as SSI/Medicaid. If the Medicare Set-Aside account is not set up inside a Special Needs Trust, the client will lose Medicaid/SSI eligibility. Therefore, in order for someone with dual eligibility to maintain their Medicaid/SSI benefits, the

MSA must be put inside a SNT. In this instance, you would have a hybrid trust which addresses both Medicaid and Medicare. It is a complicated planning tool but one that is essential when you have a client with dual eligibility.

FINANCIAL SETTLEMENT PLANNING CONSIDERATIONS

While we have discussed Mrs. Smith's public benefit preservation issues above, what about the management of her significant recovery? Should a part of it be in the form of a structured settlement? What about ongoing management of her financial affairs? Will she need help from a fiduciary such as a corporate trustee? There are no right or wrong answers to these questions. Instead, there are options for Mrs. Smith to consider and they should be presented to her so that she can make an informed decision.

The first option is to take all of the personal injury recovery in a single lump sum. If this option is selected, the lump sum is not taxable, but once invested, the gains become taxable and the receipt of the money will impact his or her ability to receive public assistance.[282] A lump sum recovery does not provide any spendthrift protection and leaves the recovery at risk for creditor claims, judgments, and wasting. The personal injury victim has the burden of managing the money to provide for their future needs, be it lost wages or future medical. Needs-based public benefits would be a lost option if a lump sum is taken as would any reduction in the premium costs for the ACA insurance programs.

The second option is receiving "periodic payments" known as a structured settlement[283] instead of a single lump sum payment.

---

282 *Id.*

283 A structured settlement is a single premium fixed annuity used to provide future periodic payments to personal physical injury victims.

A structured settlement's investment gains are never taxed,[284] it offers spendthrift protection and the money has enhanced protection against creditor claims as well as judgments. A structured settlement recipient can avoid disqualification from public assistance when a structured settlement is used in conjunction with the appropriate public benefit preservation trust. However, a structured settlement alone will never protect the disabled injury victim's needs-based public benefits.

A third option, which should always be considered, is to create a "settlement trust" as an alternative to structured settlements. Settlement trusts are typically spendthrift irrevocable trusts managed by a professional trustee and can also contain special needs provisions to allow for preservation of needs-based benefits. These trusts provide liquidity and flexibility that a structured settlement can't offer while at the same time protecting the recovery. The investment options become limitless and the trust can always be paired with a traditional structured settlement. Having a professional trustee in place that has a fiduciary duty to the client provides security for the client, and a trusted resource for life and financial management issues. In certain cases, this solution makes a lot of sense because of its ability to adapt to changing circumstances. When a disabled injury victim has needs that are not easily quantifiable or predictable, the settlement trust can adjust to the needs of the client seamlessly. When a settlement trust is paired with certain fixed income investment vehicles and a deferred lifetime annuity via a structured settlement, the client can enjoy the best of both worlds with guaranteed income for life plus sufficient liquidity.

---

284 *See* I.R.C. § 104(a)(2). *See also* Rev. Rul. 79-220 (1979) (holding recipient may exclude the full amount of the single premium annuity payments received as part of a personal injury settlement from gross income under section 104(a)(2) of the code).

WHAT CAN YOU DO TO IDENTIFY CLIENTS LIKE MRS. SMITH IN PRACTICE?

You must establish a method of screening your files to determine which of them involve those who are disabled sufficiently to warrant further planning. Once you identify a client as falling into that category, you must determine if outside experts should be consulted. As discussed earlier in relation to Medicare compliance, the easiest way to remember the process once you have identified someone as sufficiently disabled is by the acronym CAD. The "C" stands for consult with competent experts who can help deal with these complicated issues. The "A" stands for advise the client about the available planning vehicles or have an outside expert do so. The "D" stands for document what you did in relation to protecting the client. If the client decides that they don't want any type of planning, a choice they can make, then document the education they received about the issue and have them sign an acknowledgment. If they elect to do a settlement plan, hire skilled experts to put together the plan so they can help you document your file properly to close it compliantly.

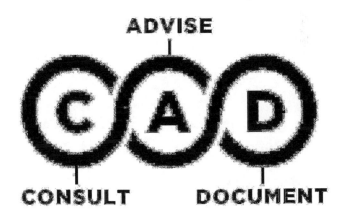

ADVISE

CONSULT

DOCUMENT

Disabled clients, especially, need counseling given the likelihood they will be receiving some type of public benefits. To prevent being exposed to a malpractice cause of action, the personal injury practitioner should understand the types of public benefits that a disabled client may be eligible for, and techniques that are available to preserve those benefits. Having this knowledge will help the lawyer identify disabled clients they may want to refer for further consultation with other experts.

WHAT DO YOU DO IF YOU REPRESENT MRS. SMITH?

When a case such as Mrs. Smith's arises, which involves the protection of public benefits or settlement assets, outside counsel is typically retained to assist with the trust devices commonly used to protect the client. Lawyers who are well versed in "settlement law" or "settlement planning" can be found and relied upon to assist with these difficult and complicated issues. The legal fees for creation of the trusts to protect the settlement monies or public benefit eligibility are normally paid for out of the injury victim's recovery. Fees can vary but the typical range at time of print is from $3,000 to $7,500 depending on the complexity of the issues.

WHAT WAS DONE TO PROTECT MRS. SMITH IN THE REAL WORLD?

On assessment of Mrs. Smith's situation, a settlement trust was created. It has two *buckets*. One bucket is an immediate fixed income portfolio of annuities that provides a high-yield stream of periodic payments to the trust that the trustee can then use to provide the client with a monthly income. The fixed income portfolio was paired with a lifetime structured settlement which was deferred to maximize return but guarantee payments for life. The second bucket is a cash reserve that is professionally managed but can be accessed when the need arises, or circumstances change. This gives the trust beneficiary the guaranteed income she needs coupled with the flexibility and liquidity that is crucial for injury victims when unforeseen needs arise.

The settlement trust created had provisions that gave the trustee discretion to move monies into the two sub-trusts identified in the trust document. These sub-trusts would allow Mrs. Smith to qualify for Medicaid/SSI as well as preserve future Medicare eligibility by utilizing special needs provisions as well as Set-Aside provisions. Until such time as eligibility was needed for public benefits, Mrs. Smith could purchase ACA coverage and make use of the settlement monies without the restrictions that accompany a Special Needs Trust or Set-Aside.

It is a win-win solution in today's complicated planning environment for settlements such as Mrs. Smith's case. One final note, while I have discussed these issues in the context of settlements, all of these considerations (with the exception of a structured settlement) can be done post-verdict. To sum it all up, complex settlements require detailed planning and creative solutions. In the next chapter, I will discuss a temporary trust called a Qualified Settlement Fund which can be an integral part of creating space and time to do the detailed settlement planning described in this chapter.

CHAPTER 18

QUALIFIED SETTLEMENT FUNDS

AN IMPORTANT SETTLEMENT TOOL FOR TRIAL LAWYERS TO UNDERSTAND

Most of this book has been dedicated to the complexities that arise when a personal injury case is settled for a catastrophically disabled client. In this chapter, I delve into a settlement tool seldom utilized but is very powerful when faced with many of the difficulties that can plague a complicated settlement. For example, imagine you just settled a personal injury case for John Doe, who is married to Jane. John has a significant brain injury and there are questions of competency. John was injured on the job but had a product's liability claim which is the part of the case you resolved. He receives both Medicaid and Medicare benefits. Medicare and Medicaid both have substantial liens along with the workers' compensation carrier. Jane has a consortium claim and there are issues of allocation of the settlement to deal with. A Medicare Set-Aside may be necessary and a SNT is a must to preserve his Medicaid eligibility. A structured settlement is being considered for part of the settlement proceeds. You, as plaintiff counsel, would like to defer taxation of your fees using a deferred compensation mechanism like an attorney fee structure.

What do you do when you settle a case like this where your client is on public assistance, there are allocation issues, settlement planning issues must be addressed, and there are liens to negotiate? Where can you "park" the money while you set up any necessary public benefit preservation trusts, determine allocation of the proceeds, figure out a financial plan, and negotiate the liens? How can you get the money from the defendant immediately without ruining the client's available settlement planning options? The answers to all these questions is to use a Qualified Settlement Fund (QSF or 468B QSF).

WHAT IS A QSF AND WHY USE ONE?

A QSF is a temporary trust established to receive settlement proceeds from a defendant or group of defendants. Its primary purpose is to allocate the monies deposited into it among various claimants and disburse the funds based upon agreement of the parties, or court order (if required). Upon disbursing all of the monies, the QSF ceases to exist.

There are many reasons to use a QSF in a complicated settlement. First and foremost, they are quite easy to establish. There are only three requirements for establishing a QSF. It must be created by a court order with continuing jurisdiction over the QSF.[285] The trust is set up to resolve tort or other legal claims prescribed by the Treasury regulations.[286] Finally, it must be a trust under applicable state law.[287] Any court, with or without jurisdiction over the matter, may sign the order creating the QSF and exert continuing jurisdiction over the trust.

---

285 Treas. Reg. §1.468B-1(c)(1).

286 Treas. Reg. §1.468B-1(c)(2).

287 Treas. Reg. §1.468B-1(c)(3).

The QSF is a temporary holding tank for the litigation settlement proceeds. It does not exist in perpetuity and is not meant to be a support trust for claimants. Instead, it exists for as long as there are allocation issues between the parties or planning that needs to be done prior to disbursement. It can exist for weeks, months, or years sometimes. There is no limit on the duration of a QSF.

A QSF may hold benefits for all parties as it relates to taxes, timing of income, and settlement planning needs. A tax-free structured settlement and a tax-deferred attorney fee structure can be properly created through the use of a QSF. The parties can influence timing of income through the use of a QSF. QSF claimants are typically not taxed on funds in the QSF until those funds are distributed (assuming the damages are taxable). A QSF also gives some extra time and flexibility for claimants to make decisions related to settlement planning issues.

The defendant receives an immediate tax deduction upon contributing the agreed-upon amount to the QSF and is typically permanently released.[288] This is a significant benefit to the defendant as normally they can't claim a deduction until the funds are received by the claimant, which can be delayed in a complicated settlement. An important point is that the tax deduction for the defendant is not impacted by when distributions actually flow out of the QSF.

The tax treatment of QSFs is uncomplicated. A QSF is assigned its own Employer Identification Number from the IRS. A QSF is taxed on its modified gross income[289] (which does not include the initial deposit of money), at a maximum rate of 35 percent.

---

288 See Treas. Reg. §1.468B-3(c).

289 Treas. Reg. §1.468B-2(b)(1).

Thus, it is taxed on accumulations to the principal from interest or dividends less deductions[290] available, which include administrative expenses.

BRIEF LEGISLATIVE HISTORY

Qualified Settlement Funds grew out of Internal Revenue Code (IRC) Section 468B. IRC Section 468B was added to the Code by Congress as part of the Tax Reform Act of 1986[291] and created Designated Settlement Funds (DSF). A DSF can be funded by one or more defendants to make settlement payments to tort claimants. The DSF was fairly limited in the way it could be utilized, and in 1993 Treasury passed regulations creating a new type of fund—Qualified Settlement Funds. There are fewer requirements to create a QSF than DSF, and a QSF can address a broader range of legal claims with increased flexibility.

The DSF and QSF were originally created for use in mass tort litigation enabling a defendant to settle a claim by depositing money into a central fund that could then settle the claims with each individual plaintiff. The defendant could walk away from the settlement fund after its creation and funding, taking a deduction for the entire settlement amount in the year it was deposited.

However, the QSF is not limited to situations involving mass torts. A Qualified Settlement Fund can be used to settle cases of any value involving multiple plaintiffs including cases involving the personal injury victim with a derivatively injured spouse, child, or parent. It can arguably be used in single plaintiff cases based upon the plain language of the Treasury Regulations implementing QSFs.

---

290 Treas. Reg. §1.468B-2(b)(2).

291 Tax Reform Act of 1986, Pub. L. No. 99-514; I.R.C. §1087(a)(7)(A), 100 Stat. 2085 (1986); I.R.C. §468B.

HOW IT WORKS

Using a 468B Qualified Settlement Fund, settlement proceeds can be placed into a QSF trust preserving the right to do a structured settlement and protecting public benefit eligibility temporarily. While the money is in the QSF, a financial settlement plan can be designed, and liens can be negotiated. Additionally, if the settlement recipient is on public benefits, the QSF avoids issues with receipt of the settlement, which could trigger a loss of public benefits. While the funds are in the QSF, there is time to create public benefit preservation trusts for the settlement recipient. A structured settlement or other financial products can then be set up to work in concert with a Special Needs Trust or Medicare Set-Aside so that the injured victim does not lose their public benefits.

IRS Code § 468B and Income Tax Regulations found at § 1.468B control the use of a QSF. These provisions provide that a defendant can make a qualifying payment to the QSF and economic performance would be accomplished, crucial for tax reasons to the defendant. Thus, the QSF trustee can receive settlement proceeds allowing the defendant a current year deduction releasing them from the case. The QSF trustee can, after receiving the settlement proceeds, agree to pay a plaintiff future periodic payments, assign that obligation to a third party, and allow the plaintiff to receive tax-free payments under IRC § 104(a) (the IRS provision excluding structured settlement periodic payments from gross income).[292] The transaction works exactly the same as it normally would when you have the defendant involved in the structured settlement transaction.

---

292 I.R.C. §104(a). Section 104(a) excludes from gross income personal physical injury recoveries paid in a lump sum or via future periodic payments. It excludes personal injury recoveries under 104(a)(2); workers' compensation recoveries at 104(a)(1) and disability recoveries under 104(a)(3).

To reiterate, there are only three requirements under 468B to establish a QSF trust. First, the fund must be established pursuant to an order of a court and is subject to the continuing jurisdiction of the court. Second, it must be established to resolve *one or more* contested claims arising out of a tort. Third, the fund, account, or trust must be a trust under applicable state law.

As for the first requirement, any court may create a QSF by court order and exercise continuing jurisdiction. It can be the court that the underlying litigation is being heard by, but it does not have to be that court. The court does not have to have jurisdiction over the tort action to establish the QSF. A QSF is "established" once a court signs the order creating it and not before. Thus, a QSF can't be funded until it is properly established.

The Treasury Regulations implementing 468B require a QSF to be established to satisfy *one or more* claims arising out of a tort.[293] However, workers' compensation claims are specifically excluded from being the basis for establishing a QSF. As long as the QSF is established to resolve a claim involving a physical injury, other than a workers' compensation claim, this requirement is easily established. The last requirement of the fund being a trust under applicable state law is simply satisfied by the proper drafting of a trust and approval by the court.

In terms of the mechanics, it is easy to establish a QSF. First, a court must be petitioned to establish the QSF. The court is provided with the QSF trust document and an order to establish the trust. Once the order is signed, the defendant is instructed to make a check payable to the QSF and the defendant is given a

---

293 Treas. Reg. §1.468B-1(c)(2). There are other claims besides torts that a QSF may be used to resolve. According to the Treasury regulations, it can be used for CERCLA claims, breach of contract, violation of law or any other claims the Commissioner of the Internal Revenue service designates in a Revenue ruling or Revenue procedure. *Id.*

cash release in return for the payment. The consideration for the release with the defendant is payment into the QSF, thus the consideration recital should reflect payment to the QSF and not the injury victim.

As for timing of distributions from a QSF, that is dependent on the agreement among claimants or as ordered by a court. For example, if the case involves minors or incompetents, the necessary court approvals would need to be obtained prior to disbursement of funds from the QSF just like they would if no QSF was involved. The QSF can provide a lump sum payment to the claimant(s); fund a SNT or MSA, pay liens, and fund a structured settlement/attorney fee structure. If a structured settlement or an attorney fee structure is funded, the QSF replaces the defendant and the transaction is consummated just as any other structured settlement would be if a defendant were involved. Upon distribution of funds from the QSF, the trustee will obtain a release from the claimants for the distributions from the QSF evidencing the fact that the distribution resolved or satisfied the claimant's claims against the QSF.

Once all funds have been distributed, the QSF ceases to exist. A court order is obtained closing the QSF and terminating the court's jurisdiction over the QSF.

ADVANTAGES OF A QSF FROM THE PLAINTIFF'S PERSPECTIVE

There are several advantages to utilizing a QSF from the plaintiff's perspective. First, funding the QSF removes the defendant and defense counsel from the settlement process. It is very much like an all-cash settlement in the eyes of the defendant. Once the trustee receives the settlement money, economic performance has occurred, and the defendant is out of the case. Second, the attorney's fees and other expenses can be paid immediately from the 468B fund. Third, the 468B trust removes the defendant from the process of allocating the settlement amounts among the various plaintiffs. Finally, and probably most importantly, the time crunch is alleviated with regard to the lien negotiations, allocations, and probate proceedings. The plaintiffs can take their time, carefully considering the various financial decisions they must make and addressing public benefit preservation issues.

The end of a personal injury case is typically a rush to settlement, which I call the "settlement time crunch." There is enormous pressure to wrap up the case quickly to get the client compensated for their injuries. However, in the rush to finalize the settlement, things may be overlooked, or important settlement planning issues may be missed. A Qualified Settlement Fund can be created to receive the settlement proceeds thereby giving everyone the time necessary to carefully plan for the future. Plaintiff counsel can get his or her fees and costs quickly. The funds are obtained from the defendant, they are released, and the client's settlement dollars can be procured quickly. The liens can be negotiated, allocation decisions can be made, public benefit preservation trusts can be implemented, and settlement planning issues, including structured settlements, can be considered. The attorney's option to structure his or her attorney fees is also preserved. The QSF is an important tool for trial lawyers to consider using.

CHAPTER 19

ATTORNEY FEE DEFERRAL

A UNIQUE OPPORTUNITY FOR CONTINGENT FEE LAWYERS TO TAX PLAN FOR TOMORROW

Over the last eighteen chapters of this book, we have examined all of the issues that catastrophically injured victims face. Now, it is time to turn our attention to the finances of a trial lawyer. An often-overlooked issue for plaintiff attorneys is the management of taxation of their own contingent legal fees. As part of the normal rhythm of their practices, many attorneys experience peaks and valleys with their own personal income. This leads to concerns for trial attorneys about the unpredictability of their own income. However, attorneys have a unique opportunity, not available to others who earn professional fees, to take their contingent legal fees and invest them on a pre-tax and tax-deferred basis to smooth out their income. Attorney fee structures and deferred compensation arrangements allow lawyers to avoid taking income all in one taxable year when they earn a large fee. However, these solutions have to be explored and decided upon prior to signing a release. While these financial products may seem complex, they are actually quite simple. Having an expert advisor who can provide you with different options is critical. The remainder of this chapter answers some frequently asked questions about deferral of contingent legal fees.

The legal foundation for this comes from a 1994 tax court decision *Childs v. Commissioner*.[294] This decision was the last time the Internal Revenue Service challenged an attorney's ability to enter into an agreement to defer their contingent legal fees. In *Childs*, US Court of Appeals for the Eleventh Circuit affirmed the tax court's ruling that attorneys may structure their fees, holding that taxes are payable on structured attorney fees at the time the amounts are received.[295] The IRS has now cited the *Childs* decision favorably and recognized it as a binding precedent in a Private Letter Ruling.[296] In that PLR, the IRS described that the "tax court held that the fair market value of a taxpayer's right to receive payments under the settlement agreement was not includable income in the year in which the settlement agreement was effected because the promise to pay was neither fixed nor secured." It went on to state that the "court further held that the doctrine of constructive receipt was not applicable because the taxpayer did not have a right to receive payment before the time fixed in the settlement agreement."

Since these are "tax-advantaged" plans, there are rules and formalities which can be a bit inflexible. It is a well-accepted tax construction that works. A lawyer, who earns a contingent fee, must decide before settlement to have his/her fee paid over time instead of taking it in a lump sum. The fee that is being deferred is paid to a life insurance company, which will agree to make future periodic payments. The decision to defer can be made at

---

294 *Childs v. Commissioner*, 103 T.C. 634 (1994) affirmed without opinion 89 F. 3d 56 (11th Cir. 1996).

295 *Id.*

296 PLR-150850-07.

any point before the settlement agreement is signed, even right up to the moment before the agreement is signed. Even though a fee has been technically earned over the course of representation of the client, the lawyer (according to tax authorities) hasn't earned the fee for tax purposes until the settlement documents are executed. An attorney has the autonomy to decide whether to defer all or part of their fee in this way.

ATTORNEY FEE STRUCTURES

Attorney fee structures are annuities, and they work very much like a nonqualified deferred compensation plan. The taxes that would be otherwise paid on the fee earned at the time the case is settled are deferred, and that money grows without tax on the growth. When distributions are made, the entire amount distributed during a year is taxable for that year. Based upon a taxpayer's tax bracket, there may be some distinct tax advantages to entering into this type of arrangement as opposed to being taxed on the entire fee in the year it was earned and investing it after tax. Depending on how much the fees are, current tax bracket rates, and any other sources of income, stretching out the payment of fees can result in a potentially smaller tax burden. This is a challenge in most professions; timing of income but controlling the realization of income is possible for attorneys. Using attorney fee structures, plaintiff attorneys can defer their fees and income taxes on those fees for personal injury cases as well as many other types of cases. An attorney fee structure allows an attorney to set up a personally tailored retirement plan without the monetary and age restrictions or other drawbacks of a qualified plan. The attorney can defer taxes on his or her fees as well as the interest that those fees earn until the year in which a distribution is actually received from the fee structure.

The fee structure can help a lawyer avoid the highest tax brackets by leveling off income spikes due to large fees and spreading the income out over several years. An attorney who otherwise would have an unusually high income in one taxable year, but elects to spread the income over several years, avoids paying taxes in the highest bracket. Couple the tax savings with guaranteed earnings on the deferred funds, and the benefits of an attorney fee structure become very obvious. Fee structures can be done by one attorney in a firm, without the requirement that other attorneys and employees participate, as would be the case in a qualified retirement plan. Also, there is no limit as to the amount of income deferred. By comparison, there are statutory limits to the amount one can defer in a qualified retirement plan. Even if the attorney participates in a qualified retirement plan or individual retirement account (IRA), he or she may still defer additional income through an attorney fee structure. Unlike traditional retirement plans, there is no requirement of annual deferments. A bonus is that the attorney fee structure is exempt from creditor's claims in most jurisdictions.

When an attorney fee is earned in a personal physical injury case, including mass torts, with all payments to the claimant being eligible for exclusion from taxable income under I.R.C. § 104(a)(2), or a workers' compensation case under section 104(a)(1), the same structured settlement annuities that the personal injury victim obtains can be used and the payment options are greatly expanded. A qualified assignment is done just as in the case of the personal injury victim. Attorney fee structures can also be done on fees from cases that are not personal physical injuries under section 104 (a)(2). These include fees from cases based on claims of discrimination, sexual harassment, employment litigation, defamation, wrongful imprisonment, wrongful termination, other non-physical personal injuries including emotional distress, punitive damages, bad faith, breach of contract, and construction defects, to name several.

Since fee structures are pre-tax and tax-deferred investment vehicles, a major benefit is the compounding effect of deferring payments over longer periods of time. The longer an attorney waits for payments or the longer the duration of the distribution term, the better the financial result and possibly the tax result as well. Payments can start right away, but don't have to. They can be deferred for any length of time and then can be paid out over a duration of years or for life. There are almost infinite possibilities in terms of the different types of arrangements that can be set up.

While structuring 100 percent of every contingent fee earned probably doesn't make sense or even a percentage of every fee, there are some unique benefits to doing so that shouldn't be ignored. A systematic approach to structuring a portion of every fee can lead to a very attractive end result when an attorney wishes to retire. For example, if an attorney took 15 to 25 percent of every contingent fee earned and deferred it out to retirement, then they would have taken advantage of the benefits of a stable retirement income, estate planning advantages, and tax benefits that most people in the workforce can't achieve. With the unpredictability of the contingent fee law practice and life in general, you don't want to rely on any one solution for retirement, and so exploring fee structures is one way to hedge against the uncertainties.

There are some key reasons to do an attorney fee structure:

1. It is a pretax investment in a guaranteed high-yielding tax deferred annuity.
2. Deferring compensation over time results in less money being lost to taxes.

3. Application of AMT can potentially be avoided.
4. Gives you custom cash flow management and allows you to tailor your own income stream.
5. Structured fees have enhanced protection from creditors, judgments, and divorce decrees.

There are some frequently asked questions related to structured attorney fees.

- Does the personal injury victim have to structure a portion of their settlement before the attorney fee can be structured? No. The claimant can take 100 percent cash and the attorney fee can still be structured.
- How does fee structuring work? Structuring an attorney fee works very similar to structuring the victim's settlement. The most important thing to remember is you can't take receipt of the fees.
- Why structure an attorney fee in a fixed interest rate annuity? Every portfolio should have some portion of the investments in fixed income. An attorney fee structure is a fixed income investment but unlike all others an attorney can make, the fee structure is a pre-tax investment. Whether a fee structure is appropriate for you will depend on a variety of factors, including your age, health, risk tolerance, retirement goals, tax bracket, as well as your current and long-term needs. However, structuring your attorney fees could provide beneficial tax relief as well as secure and stable tax-deferred income up to, and including, your lifetime.
- Can I receive the same types of income streams the victim can with their settlement proceeds? Yes, you can have lifetime benefits. You can have a "period certain" for a defined amount of time or a future lump sum payment as well as a series of lump sum payments. You can select immediate or

deferred payments. You can have multiple income streams, such as lifetime payments coupled with lump sum payments.

- Can I only structure contingent fees from a personal physical injury or wrongful death settlement? No. You can structure contingent fees from nearly any type of settlement. Companies have developed innovative products to expand the availability of attorney fee structures.
- What do I need to do to prepare for structuring my attorney fees? You should negotiate the inclusion of the fee structure when settling the case, since the creation of a tax-deferred fee structure *does* require the cooperation of the defendant, similar to when the victim's settlement is structured.

While the foregoing discussion focused on "fixed" attorney fee structure annuities, there are two other potential options that are available. First, there is an equity indexed attorney fee structure product. The equity indexed attorney fee structure ties the return to the S&P 500 Index. If the index is up, your payments increase. If the index is flat or negative, there is no decrease. So, no downside risk, only upside. The upside though is limited to a maximum ceiling of 5 percent. As the payments increase, they lock and you can only go up, never down. This type of product provides more upside potential than the traditional "fixed" fee structure while still remaining conservative. Second, there is a "nonqualified" attorney fee structure. The products in this type of structure involve an "offshore" assignment to achieve tax-deferral based on international tax treaties. Instead of using an annuity as the funding vehicle, these are open architectures allowing the attorney to use his own financial advisor to select appropriate investments, which typically include stocks, mutual funds, ETFs, bonds, and other investments. These types of products are similar to the deferred compensation plans described immediately below, since there are more available investment options but inherently have some additional risk due to the off-shore assignment. As with all of the decisions associated with fee deferral, you should consult with your own tax advisors to determine what is most suitable.

DEFERRED COMPENSATION PLANS FOR ATTORNEYS

A non-annuity deferred compensation arrangement is another mechanism that trial lawyers can use to invest the contingent legal fees they earn on a pre-tax and tax-deferred basis. Like Fortune 500 executives who defer their compensation, you can defer all or a portion of your fees until you are ready to start receiving them. Using this kind of solution, you have flexibility with investments as well as more control over the timing of income. For example, if you wanted to defer a $500,000 fee in the current taxable year by splitting the fee plus the investment gains into twenty quarterly payment buckets, you could do so. Thirteen months prior to any scheduled quarterly payment, you can elect to withdraw it. However, if you don't need the payment, the payment bucket will automatically roll forward to the end of the line. By laddering payments in this way, you can effectively manage your cash flow and better control the timing of taxation.

From a legal tax perspective, fee deferrals are subject to the same body of tax rules that govern Nonqualified Tax-Deferred Compensation (NQDC). So, this means that the deferrals must avoid the application of the constructive receipt and economic benefit doctrines. NQDC has been used for decades by Fortune 500 companies as a way to attract, retain, and further compensate their top-level executives. These deferred compensation plans rely upon the same decisions as attorney fee structures, *Childs*. Since the legal underpinnings are the same and are well established, the risk is relatively similar to attorney fee structure annuities.

CONCLUSION

In summary, attorney fee deferral solutions allow a plaintiff lawyer to not only defer receipt of (and tax on) fees until received, he or she can have the deferred fees invested, and have the income produced from it also taxable over time rather than immediately. A lawyer may want to consider deferring fees as part of his or her own income tax planning, financial planning, and estate planning. Tax deferral mechanisms for lawyers are a great way to smooth out those income spikes caused by larger fees or just take better control over timing of income. Due to the variety of options, there is likely something that will best suit an attorney's needs and investment preferences. Attorneys should explore these options to take back control of the timing of income.

CHAPTER 20

CONCLUSION

Issues that arise at the resolution of a personal injury case are an area of specialty all unto itself. There are so many legal nuances and issues that can arise which require detailed knowledge related to a variety of laws. Without the time and focus on these issues, they can be missed, and mistakes made by even the most talented trial lawyers. The ability to find and determine potential solutions to problems that can arise at settlement is critical for the client and the attorney.

As discussed throughout this book, it is critically important to consult with experts regarding the complicated issues that arise at settlement, provide counsel and advice to your client, and then document your file regarding what was done. The CAD acronym is the shorthand way to remember this for every case you handle for a disabled injury victim. Finding experts in these key areas to turn to for consults is the best way to avoid malpractice given the ever-changing and evolving nature of this area of the law.

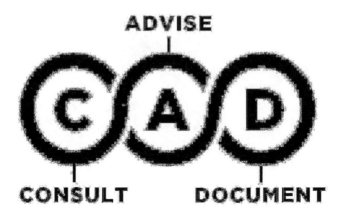

The following table summarizes many of the important issues that need to be addressed for disabled clients.

PUBLIC BENEFIT PRESERVATION PLANNING CHART FOR PERSONAL INJURY SETTLEMENTS

Those receiving government assistance need special planning to avoid disruption of benefits. The chart immediately below describes in summary fashion the different types of benefits and generally their asset sensitivity.

PUBLIC BENEFIT PROGRAM	CRITERIA	ASSET/INCOME SENSITIVE	PLANNING SOLUTION	LIEN
SSI (Supplemental Security Income)	Disabled, blind, or over age 65 AND meets income/ asset test	YES	SNT or PSNT	NO
Medicaid—Adult (Disability Based)	Disabled or over age 65 AND meets income/asset test	YES	SNT or PSNT	YES Ahlborn
Medicaid—Child (Family Related, Non Disability)	Unique financial criteria per program Settlement may not be countable	MAYBE but GENERALLY NO	N/A	YES CAN BE HMO
SSDI (Social Security Disability)	Disabled with sufficient quarters* of work history to be fully insured	NO	N/A	NO
Medicare	Disabled or over age 65 with sufficient quarters* of work history to be fully insured	NO	MSA should be considered	YES
SNAP (Supplemental Nutritional Assistance Program)	Family income/ asset test, work requirements, criminal history assessment (varies by state)	YES	SNT or PSNT	BCRC or MAO
Section 8 (Housing)	Family income test, eviction/criminal history assessment (varies by state)	YES	SNT or PSNT	NO
VA	Service requirements (self/ spouse/parent), plus certain age/disability requirements and income/asset tests for some programs	Maybe (Needs-based pensions: Yes; Disability/death compensation: No)	SNT or PSNT	NO

*Required work quarters is dependent upon when a person becomes disabled. Refer to https://www.ssa.gov/pubs/EN-05-10029.pdf.

The ability to spot the issues presented by the different government benefit programs, accompanying liens, and potential planning tools is vital to ensure against making mistakes that could prove very costly down the road. As I discussed previously, when it came to ethical responsibilities and malpractice risks, this area is ripe for potential claims against a trial lawyer. In the first chapter, I opined that if a disabled client is not given advice about how to protect their recovery, they could suffer significant damages that can be proven in a subsequent legal malpractice case. To avoid future liability, the personal injury lawyer should hire settlement experts to protect their clients and themselves. If clients refuse advice or options to protect their recovery, you should document your file that they have been advised of their options and understand what they are giving up. If your client is given all of the options and signs a waiver/acknowledgment, then you have at least properly documented the file, so if there is a subsequent legal malpractice claim, they can offer evidence of the advice given. In the end, that is the "art of settlement compliance." Education is key. Educate yourself on the issues and educate your client about matters of the law that relate to their settlement.

ACKNOWLEDGMENTS

Taking my twenty years of industry experience and distilling it down into a book hasn't been an easy endeavor. However, it has been a rewarding experience that has allowed me to reconnect once again with my passion for writing about what I do day in and day out! I want to thank my long-time colleague, Josh Pettingill, who always encouraged me to write a book on this subject.

Without the love and support from my peers and team at Synergy Settlement Services, this book would never have been possible. The experiences I have had working with everyone in the company and working with our talented trial lawyer clients has given me the inspiration to write my first book. I need to thank my peers at Synergy who helped with reading and editing content. Specifically, Dan Alvarez, Brittany Schott, Teresa Kenyon, and Simonetta Carrel-Knapp.

Lastly, and probably most importantly, I would like to thank my family members who did a lot of heavy lifting helping me to edit this book. Thank you, Etta Lazarus, my mother, and Lindsay Tremblay, for your help and support.

ABOUT THE AUTHOR

JASON D. LAZARUS is the founder and chief executive officer of Synergy Settlement Services. Synergy offers healthcare lien resolution, Medicare secondary payer compliance services, pooled trust services, settlement asset management services, and structured settlements. He is also a founding principal and president of Multi-Claimant Solutions which offers lien resolution and MSP compliance services for mass torts. Lastly, he is the managing partner and founder of the Special Needs Law Firm, a Florida law firm that provides legal services related to public benefit preservation, liens, and Medicare Secondary Payer compliance.

Prior to joining the Synergy team, Mr. Lazarus was the president of a national settlement planning firm. Before that, he spent ten years assisting injury victims as a settlement planner. Prior to starting his settlement planning practice, Mr. Lazarus practiced as a medical malpractice and workers' compensation attorney in Orlando, Florida.

Jason received his B.A. from the University of Central Florida and his JD with high honors from Florida State University. He received his LLM in elder law with distinction from Stetson University College of Law. Mr. Lazarus is a Medicare Set-Aside Consultant certified by the International Commission on Healthcare Certification.

He has had his written work published by AAJ's *Trial Magazine, Florida Justice Association Journal, The Florida Bar Journal, NAELA Journal, ElderLaw Report, Exceptional Parent, The Employee Advocate, News* and *440 Report* and *The Journal of Transnational Law & Policy*. He has presented on relevant topics for the American Association for Justice, Southern Trial Lawyers Association, Florida Justice Association, Florida Conference of Circuit Judges, Florida Workers Advocates, Workers' Compensation Section of the Florida Bar, Mass Torts Made Perfect, Lorman Educational Seminars, and countless local trial lawyer groups.

Jason's written work has been cited as authoritative on Medicare compliance by the Florida Supreme Court in the landmark collateral sources Joerg opinion and by the United States Southern District Court. He has also been either a consulting or testifying expert on the issue of collateral sources in many cases.

He is a member of the Florida Bar, Florida Justice Association (Eagle Member), American Association for Justice, National Academy of Elder Law Attorneys, Academy of Special Needs Planners, Society of Settlement Planners (Past President), and the National Alliance of Medicare Set-Aside Professionals.

.

Made in the USA
Middletown, DE
28 October 2020